Leading
the
Learning

A Field Guide for
Supervision and Evaluation

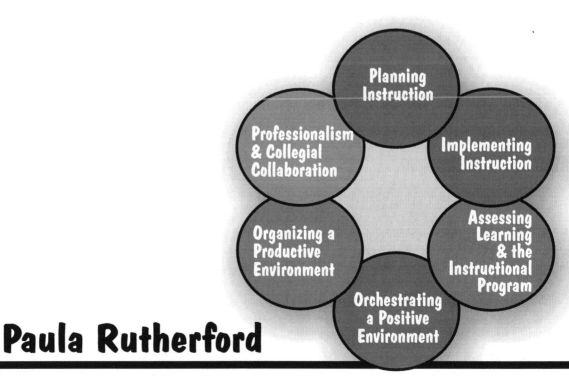

Planning
Instruction

Professionalism
& Collegial
Collaboration

Implementing
Instruction

Organizing a
Productive
Environment

Assessing
Learning
& the
Instructional
Program

Orchestrating
a Positive
Environment

Paula Rutherford

Just ASK Publications, Alexandria, Virginia

Leading the Learning
A Field Guide for Supervision and Evaluation

Published by Just ASK Publications & Professional Development
2214 King Street
Alexandria, Virginia 22301
Toll Free 1-800-940-5434
FAX 1-703-535-8502
email info@justaskpublications.com
www.justaskpublications.com

The **Leading the Learning: A Field Guide for Supervision and Evaluation** CD-ROM includes templates and exemplars for your use. Please see copyright statement included with CD-ROM for duplication rights.

All Web links in this book were correct at the time of the publication date but may have become inactive or were changed. The publisher will check the accuracy of links at the time of each subsequent printing. Should you find a link that is changed or no longer available, please send an email to info@justaskpublications.com with updated information. Please include the link, the book title, and the page number.

Printed in the United States of America
ISBN 13: 978-0-9663336-7-1
Library of Congress Control Number 2003094985
10 9 8 7 6

Table of Contents

Acknowledgments

I would like to thank the following people who have taught me so much and have greatly influenced my thinking:

Jenni Luby, former Director of Professional Development, and the Supervisory Process Team of District 220, Barrington, Illinois, who permitted me to explore with them the possibilities of a differentiated supervision and evaluation process focused on student learning and teacher reflection and growth.

Marcia Baldanza, former Principal, the SBE Teacher Leader Cadre, and staff of Patrick Henry Elementary School, Alexandria City Public Schools (ACPS), Alexandria, Virginia, who provide a role model of a professional learning community and continue to invite me to be a part of that community.

Tom Garcia, Assistant Superintendent for Human Resources, June Chapman, Director of Human Resources, Brenda Kaylor, Director of Professional Development, the Supervision and Evaluation Task force, the pilot participants, the induction coaches, and the leadership and teaching staff in St. Vrain Valley School District, Longmont, Colorado, whose rigorous work integrating supervision and evaluation into the fabric of professional life and wise counsel on how to use this process to promote the learning and growth of novice teachers is ongoing.

Linda Dinnocenzo, Assistant Superintendent for Instructional Services, the leadership team, and the teaching staff of West Irondequoit Central School District, Rochester, New York who have provided me an incredible fourteen year learning lab on maintaining an unwavering focus on student learning and using data to inform practice.

The ASK Group consultants who continue to discover new possibilities and push my thinking by asking the hard questions.

And reaching back in time, the professional developers from the Office of Staff Development and Training (OSDT), the administrators, the peer observers, and all others involved in Fairfax County Public Schools' (FCPS), Virginia, with whom I worked in the creation and implementation of The Teacher Performance Evaluation Program (TPEP) in the 1980's.

A special thanks to David Rutherford, Louise Thompson, Donovan Goode, Mike Rutherford, Larry Oakley, and Susan Maney who all contributed in significant ways to getting to press.

Introduction

This Field Guide is designed for use by supervisors of teachers and student teachers; coaches and mentors; and by classroom teachers at all stages of professional development.

The research and examples in this book are derived from the work of ASK Group members with school districts while creating or revising the supervision and evaluation processes. It also includes data from the Group's interactions with educators as they implemented induction programs, trained teacher leaders, and created professional learning communities. Educators who are working to understand and implement teaching, learning, and leading in a standards-based environment are finding that it is essential that all initiatives be aligned. They also find that the supervision and evaluation process must be embedded in the daily lives of educators, rather than being a series of events held to meet contractual obligations.

The ASK Group, in hundreds of discussions with classroom teachers, and those charged with the supervision and evaluation of teaching and learning, found widespread agreement that the supervision and evaluation process, as it has been implemented, does little to promote teacher growth and student learning. In fact, those interviewed agree that teachers prepare for scheduled classroom observations the way American families prepare for Thanksgiving dinner. For one special day, families prepare and serve food they do not eat any other day of the year. Then they present that food in a setting that is not part of the daily dining experience and with accompaniments rarely used.

That is the same way teachers often prepare and present their work in the formal observation process. In order for supervisors and mentors to know what goes on in classrooms, or in family dining practices, they need to partake on a regular basis and gather multiple forms of data in order to identify trends or patterns over time. This would require well-established and understood standards, clearly and mutually understood sets of criteria, systems for gathering and analyzing the effectiveness or efficiency of our practice, as well as feedback loops designed to further self-assessment and self-adjustment.

The other strong influence for developing this book was the extensive research base on best practice in classroom assessment and the strongly held belief that best practice in assessment of teaching and learning closely parallels best practice in classroom assessment.

Now let's go to work making a difference with this time consuming process that has incredible possibilities not yet realized!

Leading
the
Learning
The Cultural Contexts

The Contexts

What Do Schools Look Like...?
Collaboration and Job Embedded Learning
Data Driven Discussions and Decisions
Coaching and Mentoring for All
The Supervision and Evaluation Process

This section explores the cultural contexts and professional practices that influence the impact that supervision and evaluation processes can have in promoting the growth and development of students, teachers, and leaders. The essential questions addressed are:

- What do schools look like when they are organized around a commitment to the achievement of high standards by all students?

- What is my role in creating, implementing, and maintaining such a school?

- What is the role of the supervision and evaluation process in promoting teacher growth and student learning?

1

What DO schools look like...

when they organize around a commitment to the achievement of high standards by ALL students?

This question, the essential question of our work, is posed in a landmark publication entitled **Standards: From Document to Dialogue**, published by WestED. Kate Jamentz, in the chapter titled **"A Need for A New Mental Model"**, makes a compelling case that the answer does not begin with teacher classroom performance, but rather with student performance. This focus on student learning matches the thinking put forth by Ralph Tyler in 1943 in **Basic Principles of Curriculum and Instruction,** Madeline Hunter's construct of teaching to mastery objectives, Grant Wiggins and Jay McTighe's work with **Understanding by Design**, as well as the work of many others. What makes this the essential question is that it forces us to ask ourselves, **"What is MY role in such a school?"** Using a mental model that focuses on student learning, rather than on teacher behaviors, can dramatically change the way we think about the work of instructional leaders.

If student learning is really the goal, all teacher decision making and behaviors are viewed through the lens of what they need to know, do, and believe to make it happen. The primary questions addressed here focus on the role of instructional leaders, such as school and district administrators, curriculum specialists, professional developers, mentors, and coaches, in providing the pressure and support needed to help teachers examine their belief systems about themselves and the learners, acquire the necessary knowledge, and develop the required skills to put the **ALL** in all students.

Before we add new structures, we need to examine the school and school district structures already in place to see how we might use them more effectively to promote teacher growth and student achievement. Regularly scheduled meetings, induction programs, and the supervision and evaluation process have yet to be used to their fullest potential because they are not aligned with each other or with the interviewing and hiring process, school improvement plans, and professional growth plans. These processes are often seen as separate entities and the persons responsible for each of them may not interact with each other to align and integrate efforts in the interest of student learning. Such alignment may well free up time and energy to engage in new collaborative practices.

What DO schools look like...
when they organize around a commitment to the achievement of high standards by ALL students?

In Barrington, Illinois, District 220, and in St. Vrain Valley School District, Longmont, Colorado, the task forces revising their system's supervision and evaluation processes are attempting to align that process with all the other district processes. Even that alignment would be in vain, however, if they did not design the supervision and evaluation process based on what they wanted students to know and do and how they wanted students to be as learners. When student learning is the beginning point of all our planning, we greatly increase the likelihood that the criteria we select and the processes we implement are more related to creating learning environments than to control and compliance of students and teachers. The focus on student learning and the alignment with other district processes should greatly increase the growth, effectiveness, and efficiency of all educators and, in turn, student achievement.

The next seven pages provide guidance for answering these questions:

● What would students be doing in such schools?

● What would teachers need to know and do to produce such learners?

● What would leaders need to know and do to support these teachers and learners?

● What structures would need to be in place to support these practices?

The rest of this section explores in-depth the practices in which we need to engage, and the contexts in which we need to do that work if we want to see the achievement of high standards by all students.

See Tool-1: Stars for materials to engage your staff around these questions.

In schools organized around a commitment to the achievement of high standards by ALL students...

Students would...

Graduate with these characteristics and habits:

- acquire and demonstrate essential knowledge, skill, and information
- possess the tools to be successful in virtually every learning venue they encounter
- identify their own strengths and needs
- establish, reflect on, and modify personal goals for learning
- use problems and mistakes as learning opportunities
- seek and use feedback to improve their learning
- become aware of the relative effectiveness of their efforts
- push themselves and others to achieve higher levels of performance

In order for our students to develop the characteristics and habits listed above, we need to give them opportunities to practice them in our classrooms across grade levels and content areas. In school these students would:

- focus on learning rather than grades
- understand the purpose of lessons
- make connections across content areas and grade levels and see the real world relevance
- move closer to assuming responsibility for their individual learning
- be knowledgeable about the expected standards, aware of their progress relative to those standards and able to plan next steps for continued learning
- be engaged in meaningful active tasks
- understand how what they are doing is related to the standards
- know the assessment procedure and criteria from the beginning
- be enthusiastic about learning
- work hard individually and well with others
- ask questions and seek information to understand the relevance and significance of assignments
- actively seek feedback
- realize that everyone is a teacher and a learner
- follow behavior standards to create positive learning situations for all students
- communicate support for learning to parents and teachers
- think about their thinking
- demonstrate confidence and the ability to take responsible academic risks
- view school and families as partners in the pursuit of academic excellence

St. Vrain Valley School District, Longmont, CO, 2002-2003

If we want students to perform in the described ways, we need **teachers** who...

- are committed to student learning
- understand the standards of learning identified by the state and the district and can translate the standards to child friendly language
- can plan instruction that provides rehearsals and practices of the knowledge, skills, and levels of understanding required for competency with the standards
- have deep and broad understanding of the subjects they teach and can identify essential understandings, key concepts, and big ideas around which to plan instruction
- create multiple pathways to learning because they realize and accept that "one size does not fit all"
- think analytically, reflectively, and systematically about their practice and learn from experience
- use both formative and summative classroom data to inform their practice
- are active and inquisitive members of learning communities no matter how successful they already are in promoting high achievement
- are not defensive about data but rather see it as a tool for increasing productivity
- ask for and provide colleagues help in the interest of increasing student learning
- see themselves as part of a preK-12 team
- consider parents as partners in the educational process, seek them out, facilitate their involvement, and use them as rich sources of information about how best to help their children learn
- model the behaviors and habits of mind they wish to cultivate in their students

---

We need teachers who know that...

"Action research is a fancy way of saying let's study what's happening at our school and decide how to make it a better place."

Emily Calhoun

If we want teachers who perform in the described ways, we need to be Leaders of the Learning who...

believe in learner-centered education and

- see ourselves as one learner in a community of learners
- view ourselves as educators first and then as administrators
- fully understand standards as important for learning
- reflect belief in SBE through language, actions, and interactions
- help everyone in school share responsibility for everyone else's learning
- let learner needs drive decisions
- see what students and staff can do as "works in progress"
- stimulate learning by sharing responsibility and accountability
- see school as a learning organization
- support missions and goals that reflect a focus on the learner

align processes in support of content standards and

- exhibit a working knowledge of standards
- understand how standards match the broader framework of the school's vision, values, mission, and improvement plan; examine how standards affect each product, project, or program
- work with staff to develop programs that integrate home, school, and community in meeting the needs of all students
- encourage and align appropriate standards-based accountability measures for staff and students through ongoing processes
- use baseline data to guide curriculum, instruction, and assessment practices in support of standards
- ensure that these efforts result in the emergence of more coherent and effective standards-based systems

provide success opportunities for all learners and

- recognize that a wide spectrum of learning opportunities is needed to meet all needs and accommodate all learning styles and intelligences
- communicate that each student is intelligent
- provide multiple ways for students to express learning, for teachers to assess students, and for students to improve their work
- use student success as a criterion for quality education

Excerpted with permission from *Essential Roles and Responsibilities within a Standards-Based Education System*, developed by the SBE Design Team, Centennial BOCES, Longmont, CO, 1998

If we want teachers who perform in the described ways, we need to be Leaders of the Learning who...

- review student's work to understand what happens in classrooms
- give continuous and immediate performance feedback to staff
- provide resources so there are "no excuses" for learners
- provide professional development so that teachers can help all students learn, including opportunities for educators to share what they know about how students learn best

are reflective & use data to influence policies & practices and

- widen sources of data by including anecdotal data as well as "hard" data such as standardized text scores; widens quantitative data through scores on standards-based problems, presentations of learning, attendance, turnover; widens qualitative data by looking regularly at student work, especially "best effort" work
- ask hard questions about student achievement data; why do some students meet standards? Why is the performance of other students less than adequate? What are WE going to do about it?
- analyze data by looking for patterns, themes, trends, gains, losses, and sudden changes
- analyze data on individual and group levels
- read common text with staff and collaboratively identify implications for practice.
- sponsor self-study groups
- know what happens in classrooms--what the standard is, what the content and objectives are, how these relate to learner ability, and where the group is and why

Practice stewardship in support of standards and

- value and encourage shared leadership, responsibility, and decision making in recognition of individual and collective commitment to student learning
- encourage meaningful, effective, and productive partnerships and collaboration
- understand the need for and elicit community involvement in partnerships with the school
- recognize the need to make sure that everyone has a role in defining the school, and that people need to do meaningful work
- communicate effectively; fully values and focus on understanding all the voices in the community
- identify and clearly articulate commonly held community beliefs

Excerpted with permission from *Essential Roles and Responsibilities within a Standards-Based Education System*, developed by the SBE Design Team, Centennial BOCES, Longmont, CO, 1998

In Schools Committed to the Achievement of High Standards...

- there is a culture of **collaboration and job-embedded learning** focused on increased student learning
- there is a norm that educators act on what they learn; **"IT'S MY JOB"** is the appropriate bumper sticker for those educators who feel responsible for the learning of not only all students but all the adults as well

In order to move a school toward this ideal, leadership has to take responsibility for creating the context in which this could be possible. These tips capture ten significant issues we need to consider.

Top 10 Tips for Leading the Learning in a Standards-Based Environment

- Begin with the End in Mind: Achievement of High Standards by All Students
- Keep Energy and Time Focused on Teaching and Learning...Always Ask Not Only is This a Good Lesson but ...is This the Right Lesson?
- Clearly Articulate and Communicate Expectations for Teachers and Learners
- Engage in, Model, and Promote Collaborative Practice
- Develop School Structures That Support Learning for Students and Educators...Support and Participate in Job-embedded Staff Development
- Publicly Gather and Analyze Data...Make Data Driven Decisions
- View the Supervision and Evaluation Process as One-on-One Staff Development
- Constantly Refine and Expand Your Repertoire of Consulting, Collaborating, and Coaching Skills
- Recognize and Celebrate Growth and Accomplishments
- Lead with Soul!

> "...team learning is not the same as team building. The latter focuses on creating courteous protocols, improving communication, building stronger relationships, or enhancing the group's ability to perform routine tasks together. Collaborative team learning focuses on organization renewal and a willingness to work together in continuous improvement processes."
>
> **Rick DuFour**

Professional Learning Communities

A professional learning community is...

- a school with a shared mission, vision, values, and goals
- collaborative teams
- ongoing discussion about current reality and best practices
- commitment to continuous improvement
- results oriented

Schools Must...

- focus on learning, not teaching
- address these three key questions
  - ➤ **What do we expect students to learn?**
  - ➤ **How do we know if they have learned it?**
  - ➤ **How do we respond if they don't learn?**

Background Information

- In the 1990s, 1,400 schools were in involved in the restructuring process for five years or longer.
- Most showed no change.
- Those that did improve were professional learning communities.
- The most promising strategy for sustained, substantive school improvement is building the capacity of school personnel to function as a professional learning community. The path to change in the classroom lies within and through professional learning communities.

Considerations

- In a professional learning community, the adults accept learning as the fundamental purpose for the school and, therefore, are willing to examine all practices in light of their impact on learning.
- Staff members are committed to working together to achieve a collective purpose. They cultivate a collaborative culture.
- In a professional learning community, staff members find the time to address the three key questions cited above.

Bruce Oliver, ASK Group consultant and Principal, Thoreau Middle School, Vienna, Virginia, used this informational sheet to introduce his staff to professional learning communities. This is an example of a principal engaging in and promoting collaborative practice and putting in place school structures that support the learning of students and educators.

Collaboration and Job-Embedded Learning

As suggested in the **Top Ten Tips for Leading the Learning in a Standards-Based Environment** presented on page 9, supervisors who view the supervision and evaluation of competent teachers as an opportunity for collaboration and one-on-one professional development will find that the **structures listed here as formats for collaboration and job-embedded learning also appear on their list of data sources for supervision and evaluation.** As a result, many of the ways to structure job-embedded learning listed below are presented in the section entitled **Methods of Data Collection.**

- Instructional Focus for Meetings: pages 12-32
- Learning Walks: pages 34-39
- Peer Review of Plans & Products: pages 163-166
- Planning & Reflective Journals: pages 157-158
- Dialogue Journals: page 157
- Focus/Study Groups: page 34
- Book Clubs: page 33
- Learning Clubs: page 33
- Group Problem Solving
- Cognitive Coaching
- Case Studies
- Role Playing of Difficult Situations
- Analysis of Videotaped Teaching & Learning Episodes: page 27
- Observations for "Peer Poaching" & "Peer Coaching": pages 39-40
- Co-teaching: page 97
- Demonstration Teaching
- Expert Coaching
- Presentations by Internal & External "Experts"
- On-Line Chat Rooms
- Action Research: pages 41-44
- Data Analysis: pages 154-156
- Looking At Student Work: pages 45-50
- 3-D Teams: page 48
- Mentoring Relationships for All: pages 51-55
- Collaborative Teams: Grade Level, Subject Area, Vertical: page 56
- School Improvement Teams Focused on Teaching and Learning
- Teacher Leader Cadres: Building In-House Capacity: pages 57-61

Masterful and Meaningful Meetings

Planning for faculty, department, team, or committee meetings involves the same process as planning instruction for the year, the unit, or the lesson. The questions to consider are essentially the same. As the meeting planner, ask:

- **What do I want those at this meeting to know and be able to do as a result of attending and participating?**
- **How will we know when they/we are successful with those outcomes?**
- **What needs to occur at the meeting and following the meeting in order to move toward successful completion of the outcomes?**
- **How will we use data to determine next steps?**

When these essential questions provide the focus for meetings, it is no longer possible to "lead" meetings that address primarily administrivia and/or a series of unrelated agenda items.

To assess how well focused and organized the meetings you lead are, use the following guidelines to plan, to self assess, and to get feedback from meeting attendees about the effectiveness of the meeting.

- **The purposes of the meeting were clearly communicated**
- **The activities at the meeting were aligned with the purposes**
- **The meeting was structured so that all participants were meaningfully engaged**
- **All the people who needed to hear the information and/or be involved in the decision making process were in attendance**
- **The topics under discussion needed face-to-face interaction and could not have been handled electronically or on paper**
- **The decision making process and ultimate decision makers were clearly identified**
- **Essential data and rationales for action were used**
- **The issues discussed, studied, and/or decided at previous meetings and addressed between meetings were discussed and integrated as appropriate**

When you hear...
"Not Another Meeting!"
Use the ones already scheduled in more productive ways!

Translating active learning structures listed below into learning structures for adults yields quick ways to build dialogue, discussion, and conversations into faculty, department, team, and committee meetings.

In addition to facilitating active engagement of adults, using these structures gives you a chance to model the processes for staff. After debriefing the content under discussion be sure to always ask these process questions:

- **How might you use this active learning strategy in your classroom?**
- **How is this active learning strategy like a strategy you already use?**

At the next meeting, ask staff members to share how they used the structure in their instructional program and how it promoted student learning.

Anticipation/Reaction Guide

Purposes

- To establish a purpose for reading
- To access prior knowledge
- To help participants reframe their thinking as necessary
- To introduce new processes, procedures, or programs
- To surface strongly held beliefs that may be challenged by the new information to be presented

Process

- Prepare a series of statements related to the reading or other input source.
- Have staff members, before reading, indicate whether they think the statement is true or false.
- Have staff read the selection or watch the video or demonstration.
- Have staff, after reading, answer the same questions again.
- Have staff discuss where they found the information that changed their thinking. what surprised them, and the implications for practice.

Framing the Learning
Anticipation/Reaction Guide

Before Reading   **After Reading**

_____ 1. Accessing prior knowledge helps level the playing field for learners.   1._____

_____ 2. It is extremely difficult for students to give up misconceptions.   2._____

_____ 3. Providing exemplars for the learning of processes looks like what Madeline Hunter called guided practice.   3._____

_____ 4. Students in primary grades do not need to be informed of the learning standards.   4._____

_____ 5. Student achievement increases when students know what excellent work looks like.   5._____

Note: 4 is false.

Anticipation/Reaction Guide was developed by Bean and Peterson.

AAA-An Awesome Array of Articles

Purposes

- To provide focus and time for professional dialogue around significant ideas
- To maximize amount of information to be introduced and minimize the amount of preparation time of individuals
- To build in peer pressure through interdependence
- To prepare for follow up discussions, reflections, or action plans by individuals, teams, or staffs

Process

- To prepare for this discussion, ask staff members to read one of four or five selected articles on a designated topic and complete a **3-2-1** summary reflection on their reading. See explanation of **3-2-1** on page 28 and **Tool-9: 3-2-1**.

- At the meeting have them take their article and their **3-2-1** summary and participate in an **expert group meeting** to discuss their learning and reactions to the selected article. The person who has the next birthday can be the facilitator who ensures that all voices are heard during the discussions.

- Allow twenty to twenty-five minutes for expert group discussions.

- At the end of the discussion time, provide each group with a piece of chart paper and markers so that they can create a summary of the key points from their reading and discussions. They may elect to create a picture, a graphic organizer, a bulleted report, a poem, etc. Do not distribute chart paper until the close of discussions so that all are engaged throughout the discussion.

- **Chart preparation** should not last more than ten to fifteen minutes.

- Post the charts and then have staff members participate in a **Gallery Walk** where they review the printed summaries. See page 21 for an explanation of a **Gallery Walk.**

- Have a spokesperson present a three minute commercial for the article as a summary of both the content and the group's reactions.

Possibilities

- Articles in differentiation
- Articles on assessment
- Articles on professional learning communities
- Articles on homework

See Tool-9: 3-2-1

Collegial Collaborators

Purposes

- To promote interaction of staff members across the group
- To pause for processing a la **10:2 Theory** (See page 87 in **Instruction for All Students**.)
- To build in movement
- To structure one-on-one conversations
- To cause participants to share their own perspectives on an issue and to learn about the perceptions and thinking of others.

Process

- Staff members can self select a discussion partner with the stipulation that the person not be in their department, grade level, hallway, etc.
- An option is to use the **Think-Pair-Share** process in which individuals think, and perhaps jot down some thoughts, about the topic and then meet with a partner to discuss their own ideas. (See page 112 in **Instruction for All Students**.) Random sharing can be structured so that those who are asked to share in large group share what their partner said rather than repeating what they said. This promotes better listening during the paired discussions.
- To build in movement, have the partners stand together as they hold their discussion. If there is a need for tightly structuring the discussion, have one person talk for one minute and then the other for one minute with the conversation closed by having each summarize what the other said for thirty seconds. The time for these processing discussions is generally brief; two to four minutes is the norm.

Possibilities

- Have staff members sign up with multiple partners to meet with individually over time.

- **Use the Collegial Collaborator Tool** or another graphic with slots for ten to twelve "appointments." At each slot, two staff members record each other's name. This sign-up period takes about four to five minutes and provides an efficient way for staff members to interact with many colleagues over time. See pages 99-100 in **Instruction for All Students** and pages 252-253 in **Why Didn't I Learn This in College?** for more information.

See Tool-2: Collegial Collaborators

Collegial Collaborators

Consensogram

Purpose
- To quickly capture a public graph of where people are on various issues

Process
- Select a topic or issue where there is a need to know how individuals and the group are thinking.
- List the topics or components of the issues as titles and list percentages down the left side.
- Have participants place a stick on note or a sticker dot next to the percentage that represents how much they know about or value the subject under consideration.

Possibilities
- How much you like ...?
- Predict what percentage of the group knows, thinks, likes, uses, etc. Do actual percentage in a different color note or sticker dot.
- Percentage of students achieving advanced proficiency, being referred to the office, advanced placement, in lowest quartile of standardized test, etc.
- How much do you know about...?
- How frequently do you use...?
- How much you agree with...?

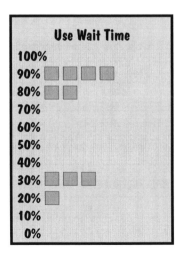

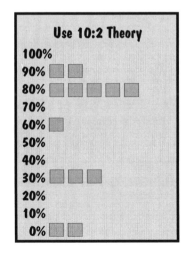

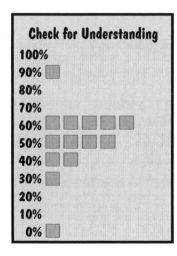

Consensus Conclusions

Purpose
- To help groups quickly build consensus while ensuring that all voices are heard.

Processes

Facts in Five
- Have staff members individually generate a personal list of the five most important variables, issues, concerns, or data sets related to the topic under discussion.
- Have participants then move into groups of five.
- Have the group of five reach consensus on the five most important facts or concepts and clarify their rationale for selecting each.
- Have each group create a chart listing their consensus decision.
- Have each group present their selections and the rationale for each selection to the larger group.
- If time is short, post the choices on the bulletin board for later examination.
- Type a list of the charted responses for further discussion or for the development of an action plan, as appropriate.

1-3-6
- Have participants follow the same sequence as in **Facts in Five**, but after they work individually, have them move to groups of three and then to groups of six.
- This format takes longer, but may be most effective if participants have little experience or success with building consensus. It also provides more opportunity for dialogue and debate.

Spend a Buck
If further consensus is needed, after the charts are posted, provide each participant with sticker dots "to spend."
- Give each one 10 dots worth 10 cents each and explain that they can spend all their dots on one point or they can divide them however they choose to include 10 cents on 10 different points.
- Have participants place their dots on the charts next to the points most important to them.
- When all have "spent their bucks," group priorities will be graphically displayed on the charts.

 Corners

Corners

Purposes

- To have staff members consider multiple, possible conflicting, causes, options, or levels of agreement on a complex topic
- To build in movement
- To promote staff discussion with those who agree, and dialogue and debate with those who hold differing views

Process

- Pose a question that has multiple answers or ask staff members to rank order several options.

- Give staff members time to consider their own thinking about the topic. Then have them move to the corner of the room that has been designated as the meeting place for all those holding the same opinion or view.

- In the corner meeting places, have staff members discuss why they think or believe the way they do. If the groups are large, have them divide into pairs or triads so that all can voice their opinions and their rationales.

- As appropriate, have selected volunteers report for their corner. Large group sharing can be oral or the corner groups can generate and share charts listing their rationales for choosing that particular answer/viewpoint.

- This exercise can be followed by presentation of new information, development of action research, and tabled for further data gathering.

Possibilities

- Importance of variables that might be used in determining master schedule, course or grade level assignments, room assignments, or co-curricular positions
- Issues related to grading
- Use of time, such as length of class periods, pull out programs, starting times
- Potential focus areas for professional development
- Relative merit of various pedagogical approaches

 Corners

Corners

Frame of Reference

Purposes
- To surface and reflect on prior knowledge or related experiences
- To point out different perspectives based on where and when one learned about or experienced something

Process
- The **topic or issue** to be discussed is placed in the center of the matted frame where a picture would be placed in a picture frame. Model using an overhead transparency.
- Ask staff members to individually jot down **words or phrases** that come to mind when they hear or see the term **pictured**. These words go in the "mat" area of their frame of reference. Model a few ideas.
- Ask them then to jot down how they came to know what they know or think...that is the sources, people, events that have **influenced their thinking.** These reactions go in the **frame** area of the graphic.
- Following the individual reflection and writing, participants are asked to share their **frames of reference** with a partner or a small group.

Possibilities
- Place the name of a student or an important player in the school community (parents, board members, school neighbors, custodians, etc.) in the center. They then jot down how this person would describe the school or an issue impacting the school community. Assigning different people different persons/perspectives can lead to powerful **in the voice of** discussions when the frames of references are completed.
- Use as an introductory and community building exercise. Staff members put their own names in the center, describe themselves and then cite those people and events that have shaped their thinking and lives.
- Supervision and Evaluation
- Block Scheduling
- Reading in the Content Areas
- Rigor/Levels of Thinking
- Performance Assessment

My Frame of Reference

What I Know

Topic

How I Know What I Know

See Tool-3: Frame of Reference

Graffiti

Purposes

- To capture the thinking and reactions of the staff to multiple ideas or aspects of the same idea
- To have staff members quickly see the opinions, reactions, or concerns of other staff members
- To have staff members process a great deal of information with movement and conversation

Process

- Write quotes, prompts, questions, or areas of concern (one to a chart) on large sheets of chart paper and post them around the room. Alternatively, you can tape 8½" x 11" sheets of paper to the middle of large sheets of chart paper.
- Have small groups of 4-5 begin work at different charts.
- Have them respond to the topic or title of the chart by writing responses or **Graffiti**, which can be short words, phrases, or graphics on the chart paper.
- After the allotted time period, have staff members move to the next chart.
- Repeat the process until all groups have reacted to all charts.
- Have staff members process the patterns, trends, and implications for their practice from what is written on the charts.

Possibilities

- Top Ten Questions for Secondary Teachers (See page 258 in *Instruction for All Students*). Place one statement on each chart and have staff members circulate to generate ideas of how they do or could do each.
- Top Ten Questions I Ask Myself When I Design Lessons (See page 36 in *Instruction for All Students*).
- See pages 35-36 for an example of how one school staff used **Graffiti** to generate **Look Fors** and **Listen Fors** in a Standards-Based Classroom.

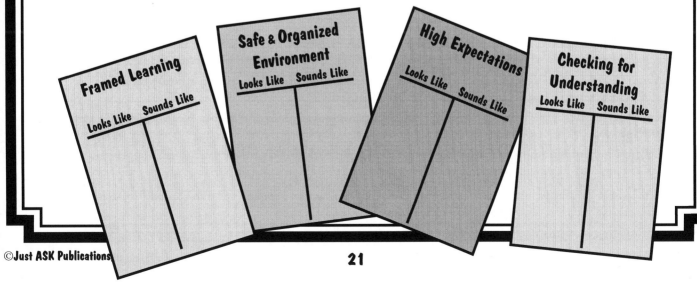

On My Mind

Purposes

- To complete an interest/issues survey
- To complete a needs assessment
- To identify high priority issues or actions
- To build consensus
- To ensure that all voices are heard

Process

Individual Reflection

Place a stack of white index cards on each table. Have staff members distribute three of the cards to each member of the table group. Have them use these cards to record questions that are **On Your Mind** related to the topic under discussion. Have them put only one question on each card. If anyone has more questions, they may use more cards.

Round One

When staff members have completed their cards, have them circulate them for three to five minutes at their own tables. Tell them that if, as they read the circulating cards, they find they are really curious about the question posed on the card, place a small dot (show example) on the card and put the card back in circulation. Have them put dots only on those that relate to an issue they see as significant. If they do not find the question listed as one of great importance, have them place the card back in circulation without a dot.

Rounds Two and Three

Allow three to five minutes of time for circulation of cards at the base table then call time and have each group pass their cards to the next table. Have them repeat the circulation process and attachment of the dots to indicate a high level of interest in the question posed. If time allows, repeat the process with a third table.

Collection

At the completion of the final round, have them place the cards in the center of their table for collection. If there is time, identify the five or six cards with the most dots and have them read aloud.

Follow-up

Analyze the data and report back to the group about the key issues, questions, or concerns that surfaced.

Scavenger Hunt

Purposes

- To review, preview, and expand a topic
- To demonstrate to staff that collectively they know a great deal about the topic under discussion
- To build in interaction and movement with a variety of people and hear different perspectives

Process

- Prepare a set of questions on a topic.
- If staff members are not already in table groups or teams, they will need to be in groups to discuss their work after the scavenger hunt.
- Have participants individually read through the questions, select one for which they will be the expert, and answer just that one on their sheets. As an alternative, you may assign a specific question to each participant or have them draw the question number out of a hat.
- You may want to initial the answers before they start the hunt to ensure that a "virus" does not spread around the room, or you may want to let participants discover and deal with any errors.
- Staff members can use all the people and materials in the room as resources to obtain the rest of the answers. They may only obtain one answer from each person they ask.
- Answers can "flow through" one person to another, but the "third party" and middle person should be prepared to fully explain the answer.
- When time is called, participants return to their table groups or teams, verify answers, and complete any unfinished answers.
- Only unresolved issues need be discussed with the entire group.

Possibilities

- See **Tool-10: Scavenger Hunt**, based on *Instruction for All Students*
- See **Tool-11** for a variation of a **Scavenger Hunt** on standards-based education.

Use these interview questions to celebrate the accomplishments of the past school year. Have staff members choose three or four questions they would like to discuss and "interview" a different colleague about each one, taking turns with the interviewing process. When the interview sessions are completed, have staff members complete **Tool-12: Now Hear This!** to capture one significant accomplishment that will be shared later in the meeting, at a future meeting, or placed on a bulletin board.

Shop Talk

Purposes
- To introduce different perspectives
- To structure **Think-Pair-Share** time
- To access prior knowledge
- To provide focus for upcoming work
- To cause cognitive dissonance

Process
- Identify a topic or situation that merits quality discussion.
- Select quotes, scenarios, or case studies that represent that topic or situation.
- Prepare different discussion cards for each faculty member.
- Distribute the discussion cards to each participant. The cards may contain the same information, related information, or conflicting information.
- Have each participant read the card and then meet with a colleague to discuss the information on the card.
- As appropriate, have partners meet with others to compare and contrast or combine information.

Possibilities
- Mix and match terms, definitions, and examples related to the discussion or reading that is to occur
- Opinions about a topic from the perspective of a student, a teacher, a parent, a community member
- Quotes about educational philosophy
- Descriptions of classroom or school events and possibilities for solving or resolving the issues
- Events that have occurred over time in the school... staff members line up in chronological order
- Types of questions
- Descriptions of school events around which staff members do a cause and effect analysis
- Formulate hypothesis about what problems or situations occurred
- Mini case studies

Sort Cards

Purposes
- To develop a sense how individuals and small groups are thinking about a topic
- To have staff members "handle" information

Process
- Staff members, working individually, generate words, and short phrases that come to mind when they think of a designated topic. They record each idea on a separate index card.
- Working in small groups, staff members:
  - share ideas
  - clarify similar ideas
  - eliminate duplicates
- Staff members sort the ideas generated by the group into categories. The categories can be created by the participants or the facilitator of the meeting.
- When the sorting and labeling is completed, the staff members take a tour around the room to observe and analyze the work of other groups. One person stays behind at the base table to answer questions.
- Groups return to tables to discuss what they observed and to revise or add new ideas/categories.
- Groups use the generated ideas and categories as a basis of future study or discussion.
- Ask staff members to do metacognitive processing; that is, have them process how they went about their thinking as they generated, sorted, categorized, labeled, and analyzed the work of others.
- Once these cards are generated, they can be used for a multitude of other purposes. Participants could sort them again later in the year to see how their thinking has changed over time.

Possibilities
- Differentiation
- Literacy
- No Child Left Behind
- Inclusion
- Use of Strategies

Stir the Faculty

Purposes

- To access prior knowledge and experiences
- To validate current best practice
- To promote collegial collaboration
- To generate comprehensive lists
- To set the stage for new learning

Process

- Provide each participant with a data collection sheet containing ten to twenty lines, or have them number their own sheets.
- Have each one write, as directed, three strategies, three reasons, three causes, three points of interest, etc., about the topic/concept to be studied. Ask them to make the third one on their list unique.
- At a signal, have them move around the room collecting/giving one idea from/to each participant. Ideas received from one person can be passed "through" to another person.
- After an appropriate amount of time, have them return to their seats. At this point, you can have them compare lists, prioritize, categorize, or select two or three they would like to try.
- At this point, they can continue with a format appropriate to the level of thinking you want them to do. They have had time to focus on the subject and to hear ideas from colleagues.
- As appropriate, create and distribute a master list of ideas.

Possibilities

- Ways we check homework
- Ways we pre-assess
- Ways we get students' attention
- Organizational systems for teacher, classroom, or students

Stir the Faculty on:

1 Your own idea

2 Your own idea

✱ 3 Your own really original idea!

4
5
6
7
8
9
10
11
12
13
14
15
16
17
18
19
20

See Tool-5: Stir the Faculty

Take Ten!

Purposes
- To provide exemplars of best practice
- To orchestrate a common teaching and learning experience around which to focus discussions
- To introduce new teaching strategies

Process
- Select 5-10 minute video clips of teaching and learning episodes that represent best practice or clips of student performances to show at faculty or department meetings
- Introduce clip with demographic and contextual information and provide a focus for viewing. Consider using one of the district professional practice criteria as the focus
- Show video clip
- Have staff members analyze and discuss according to the prompt given prior to showing the clip

Possible Video Sources
All commercial tapes can be ordered on-line.
- **The Lesson Collection** from ASCD consists of more than 20 videos ranging from 10 to 20 minutes in length. They are sold separately and clearly identified as to grade level, subject, and strategies used.
- **Principles in Action** from McREL features four schools/school districts that won the 1996 Professional Development Award from the US Department of Education for increasing student achievement as a result of the implementation of learnings from professional development.
- **Schools That Learn** from NASSP features three middle schools as exemplars of how to promote high expectations for all students. One clip features Algebra instruction; the others focus more on looking at student work.
- Annenberg markets dozens of videotapes featuring math and science education K-12. **A Private Universe**, which focuses on how student misconceptions interfere with student learning, is available from Annenburg.
- FASE Productions markets several videotapes featuring Kay Toliver, a middle school math teacher from New York City. **Good Morning, Miss Toliver** is available from FASE.
- Use videotapes of staff members and their students.

Three-Column Charts

Purposes

- To help staff members access prior knowledge
- To identify areas of interest or concern
- To aid the meeting facilitator in planning future meetings
- To track increased understanding or commitment throughout a project
- To identify areas for further research/study
- To identify areas of expertise

Process

- Use this strategy prior to, during, or at the close of any discussion. The process can be done individually, in small groups, or as a whole group.
- Announce topic and column titles; post on charts, or have staff members record in table groups.
- Record or have the table discussion facilitator record responses to the stems.
- During the brainstorming phase, emphasize getting lots of ideas rather than debating or discussing the ideas as they are generated. Debates, clarifications, and discussion of ideas occur once the brainstorming is over. Do not clarify any confusions or react in any way other than to record the data. Conflicting data may be recorded.

Possibilities

Choose any **one** of the following **sets** of column headings, or create your own.

	Validations for Current Practice	We're Working on This One	Good Idea! Haven't Tried it Yet
OR	What I Knew	What I Now Know	What I Still Don't Know
OR	What I Know	What I Don't Know	What I Wish I Knew
OR	Productive	Somewhat Productive	Unproductive
OR	Most Important	Somewhat Important	Not Important at All
OR	Almost All of Us	Some of Us	Very Few of Us
OR	Most of the Time	Some of the Time	Almost Never
OR	In Place & Functioning Smoothly	Work in Progress	Not Yet

See Tool-8: Three-Column Chart

3 - 2 - 1

Purpose

- To provide a structure for meaning making and summarizing key points in a reading, meeting, or workshop

Possibilities

- The stems for 3 - 2 - 1 can be created to match the kind or level of thinking you want staff members to do about the material being studied.

3 most important ideas you would like to discuss further

2 questions or concerns

1 implication for your practice

- At the end of a discussion, a reading, or a video participants might be asked to write and then discuss:

3 strategies you would like to try and why you think they would work well with your students

2 strategies that are similar to ones you already use

1 question you would like to ask the author or person featured in the video

- Marcia Baldanza, Principal of Patrick Henry Elementary School, Alexandria City Public Schools, Alexandria, Virginia, uses the 3-2-1 exercise following teacher candidate interviews. Applicants are asked to respond to these stems:

3 reasons you are the perfect person for this job

2 important facts about you that we did not come up in the interview

1 question or comment you have for our team

See Tool-9: 3-2-1 Tool

Ticket to Leave

Purposes

- To generate a list of what staff members thought was most significant about the information discussed during the meeting or workshop
- To have participants make personal meaning/cognitive connections with the concepts discussed

Process

- Use at the end of a meeting or when you break for lunch.
- Have participants use either their own paper, an index card, or a stick on note. Alternatively, participants could draw or tell their thinking.
- Select an appropriate stem and provide time for participants to write their responses. The stem will be determined by the topic under consideration and the kind of thinking you want them to do.
- Stand at the door and collect the notes as they leave or have them place a stick on note on the door as they leave.

Possibilities

- The most interesting/important thing you heard today and why you chose it
- As a result of today/this meeting I ...
- One reason why today's meeting may help you help more students learn more
- One question that comes to mind about the issues we discussed today
- One thing you accomplished today about which you feel a sense of pride, self-efficacy, or growth
- One action I am definitely going to take because of what I heard today

Report back to the group on patterns or trends. This models the gathering of informal assessment data.

Walk and Talk

Purposes
- To structure discussion of selected readings
- To incorporate 10:2 Theory and movement into a reading task

Process
- Select a journal article or a reading from a text, the internet, or the newspaper.
- Have two people reading the same selection pair up for the Walk and Talk process.
- The pair looks through the reading and identifies three "stopping for processing" points.
- Both readers read the first segment and then stop reading to discuss their reactions to that segment.
- The process is repeated for the remaining segments of the reading.
- At the conclusion of the process, the pairs are asked to share their overall reactions to both the content of their reading and to the walk and talk process, either in table group discussions or in large group.
- ...All this is done, of course, while taking a much needed stroll around the building or, if the weather is nice, a stroll around the grounds. Perfect for an after-school workshop or meeting!

Possibilities
- Assessment
- Reading in the content areas
- Pedagogy
- Homework
- Grading
- Second language learners

Articles/books marked with an * in **Resources and References** found in the **Appendices** section are recommended as readings.

Walking Tour

Purposes

- To introduce complex texts, provocative ideas, or discrepancies
- To emphasize key ideas of complex material
- To raise curiosity and increase speculation about a subject

Process

- **Compose five to eight charts** that represent the content material, pictorially or verbally. Use photographs of places or objects, direct quotes from the text, or other means to convey one idea per chart. **Hint:** If the tour is used to introduce complex concepts or a complex reading, isolate the primary points and create one chart for each point.
- **Post the charts** around the room and number each chart. Divide staff members into "touring groups" to fit the space and complexity of the material.
- **Assign one group per chart** as a starting point. Groups spend two to five minutes at that chart, taking notes on and/or discussing the idea presented.
- **Rotate the groups** until all groups have "toured" each chart. When staff members return to their seats, allow time for discussion and reactions.

Variations

- **Jigsaw Walking Tour -** If time to tour is limited, form groups made up of the same number of staff members as there are charts around the room (four charts means there should be four members in a group). Have group members number off and send one representative to each chart. Staff members form new groups at the charts and react. They then return to their original groups to take turns reporting on the information on each chart and their reactions to it.
- **Gallery Walk -** Charts or other visuals created by staff as a reaction to a discussion or a reading are displayed and small groups tour the charts to look for patterns or connections.

Possibilities

- Paragraphs from an article
- Components of a school improvement plan
- Any new or changed process
- Examples of student work

Beyond the Faculty Meeting

Learning Clubs

Learning Clubs are small groups of teachers who meet regularly to discuss their lives as teachers. During a learning club meeting, **each teacher takes a turn** discussing some aspect of her teaching life. In running her part of the meeting, the teacher selects one of four types of discussion:

- **Review:** The teacher asks the group to focus on an instructional strategy they have studied together and explain how it is working in each of their classes. The discussion would focus on how it worked and what they learned from their initial attempts to use the strategy.

- **Problem Solving:** The teacher presents a problem he is currently facing and asks the group for help in clarifying the problem and brainstorming possible actions to take. A structured problem solving model will yield the best results.

- **Now Hear This!** The teacher announces that she wants to use her time to either share a success story about a recent or current instructional encounter, or to complain about a dilemma she is facing. In a **Now Hear This!** session, the group members' responsibility is to appear interested and use active listening. They do not offer solutions or suggestions.

- **Lesson Design:** The teacher asks the group to help plan a lesson or unit, or to review a plan he has designed.

After a teacher has announced what kind of help he wants, and the group has focused on his issues for approximately 15 minutes, his turn ends and another teacher begins her turn by declaring what kind of session she wants. Once each group member has had a turn, the group spends five to ten minutes discussing the ideas shared during the meeting and the implications of each for their professional practice.

Book Clubs

Prior to the meeting, group members all read an article or a chapter in a jointly selected book. The meeting revolves around a discussion of the book and the implications for classroom practice. An alternative is to have each member of the group bring a different article related to a group identified issue or to have each member read a different book on a topic. Each participant then shares a review of that article/book over a series of meetings. The discussion focus is on the implications for decision making and classroom practice.

Beyond the Faculty Meeting

Focus Groups

These meetings are opportunities for educators to spend dedicated time in the discussion of classroom practice. These discussions usually include the presentation or demonstration of new strategies or the sharing of action research results. Group members might research materials, instruction strategies, or content specific methodologies. Participants might agree to experiment with an idea or approach in their own classrooms, to report back on how it worked, to analyze the results together, and then to try it again. Focus groups meet for two or more times so that they can come back together and discuss what they learned.

Learning Walks

Shared experiences around teaching practice are important for professional growth. Meetings and conferences where classroom practice is discussed are the usual forum; the reality is that we have been missing important learning labs all around us. When small groups of teachers identify a focus and then walk through their own buildings looking for evidence of that focus, the learning curve is steep, the dialogue is rich, and professional relationships are strengthened.

If those participating in a learning walk are participating in a learning club, book club, or focus group, they can make the focus of their learning walk the same as the focus of their study group. Other focuses might include areas identified in school, department, or grade level improvement plans. Mentors and novice teachers walking together can gather important data about classroom practice that can frame their discussion for months.

In large schools with multiple administrators, learning walks by administrative teams can refine and expand their repertoires and knowledge about instructional practice. When an administrator is given the assignment of supervising a grade level or department for which he does not have direct experience, a series of learning walks with a knowledgeable team leader, department chair, curriculum specialist, or other administrators with background in that arena can provide a rich learning experience.

On the following pages there are three examples of how learning walks are being used. At Patrick Henry Elementary School the SBE Teacher Leader Cadre does focused learning walks on a regular basis using the indicators identified by the entire staff. In the other two examples, the learning walks were summarized in a newsletter and distributed to all staff members.

These learning walks are conducted in exactly the same ways administrators do walk-throughs. See pages 148-153 for information on walk-throughs.

Patrick Henry Elementary School* Learning Walk
Look For's and Listen For's

Framed Learning

Looks Like:
- Standards of learning posted
- Internalized standards
- Lots of students work depicting standards learned
- Confidence and a sense of direction
- Standards guide all classroom decisions
- Objectives stated in terms students can understand
- Cloze activities
- Structured curriculum with coherence between grade levels
- Pruned textbooks
- Purposeful and focused curriculum and instruction

Sounds Like:
- Yesterday we... today we are going to...
- Students can state what they are learning and why
- Students are engaging by working in small groups (telling/sharing interests
- At the end of the unit, you will be able to...
- Students relate current learning to past learning
- Productive activity
- Students, teachers, and parents all speaking the same language

High Expectations

Looks Like:
- Syllabus/course study laid out
- Objectives posted
- Rubrics with "going beyond expectations" posted
- Positive work samples available
- Communication of expectations to parents
- Students understand what is expected
- Students think and perform "out of the box"
- Students actively engaged
- Learning styles are respected and addressed
- Students take risks and use knowledge in new ways
- Achievement charts
- Work is connected to real-life applications
- Purposeful and focused curriculum and instruction

Sounds Like:
- Clear statements of learning outcomes
- "Do your best work!"
- Productive student chatter
- Wait time for students
- "Now, how can you make it better?"
- "Just do it!"
- Children sharing their ideas
- "Look at the great idea _____ had!"
- "I did extra to earn a 5."

The staff of Patrick Henry Elementary School, Alexandria City Public Schools (ACPS), Alexandria, VA, brainstormed these indicators using the Graffiti exercise during a staff meeting.

Looks Like:

- Flexible arrangement of desks allowing for different activities
- Area is free of obstacles to ensure ease of movement and lack of injury
- Students are taking risks
- Students are sharing thoughts with one another
- Materials are clearly labeled
- Teacher can move easily from student to student
- Students understand procedures...know where to be and what to do
- Inappropriate student behavior is redirected privately
- Interactions are positive
- Students move comfortably around the room and are respectful of others

Sounds Like:

- Enthusiastic, but moderate voices
- Students sharing in small groups and with whole class
- Guided group discussion
- Respective tone
- System for students to be responsible for organizing materials
- "I can do this."
- "I have an idea to try."
- Excitement about learning
- All students participating in class activities and discussions
- Learning noise

Looks Like:

- Portfolios with exhibits
- Varied assessments
- Children using visual cues to show understanding
- Rubrics on walls
- Conversation among peers
- KWL charts
- Demonstrations
- Exit Slip. "Today I learned..."
- Graphic organizers and Venn diagrams
- Students re-teaching what they have learned

Sounds Like:

- Tell me what you think when you solve problems
- Peer tutoring
- What did you just do and why?
- How an we apply information we just learned to everyday situations?
- Students repeating or modeling what the teacher taught/said
- Can you, in turn, teach this to another?
- Reviewing
- Thumbs up, thumbs down
- "I could use the information or skill to..."
- Orally answering
- Students talking about how they are doing with the standards
- Processing and summarizing throughout the lesson

Learning Walks

To: **Parkland-Brookside Teachers**
From: **Ray, Heather, and Connie**
Re: **Learning Walk Observations**

It is evident as we walked around our buildings this week that folks are working hard to enhance the quality of the teaching and learning process. As we continued data gathering on constructivist teaching and learning, we gathered data that teachers are working to differentiate instruction on the basis of students' needs and interests, help students attach relevance to the curriculum, and structure lessons around big ideas, not small bits of information.

Here are some of the exemplary practices we observed:

- In second grade, we saw a **differentiated lesson** integrating language arts and science where students were working on specific performance indicators and using graphic organizers differentiated by readiness.

- In fifth grade, we observed **the use of literature and technology to support the mathematical concept of polygons**. Students had an opportunity to plot the coordinates of their polygons on the computer and use the data to make comparisons.

- In pre-kindergarten, students were working with a "hula hoop Venn Diagram" to **compare two science concepts; transparent and translucent.**

- In third grade, students were working with partners to create various **arrays** on chart paper and sharing their understandings of multiplication.

- Special area teachers were **integrating math and science concepts** into daily instruction.

- In grades pre-K, 1, and 2, teachers were collaborating on student management, organization, and engagement in **guided reading centers.**

- In grades 3, 4, and 5 teachers were collaborating on strategies for **processing text with understanding** in small, guided reading groups.

As we continue our hard work of helping children to construct their own meaning, let us be ever purposeful in our assessment of student learning in the context of daily classroom investigations, and continue to help students demonstrate their knowledge every day in a variety of ways.

Greece Central School District, Greece, NY

From the Doorway...
Peeks into Pedagogy

Standards-based or Standards-referenced?

The stages of being standards-based are as follows:

- Knowing that the standards exist
- Knowing where to find a copy
- Reading the standards
- Posting the standards
- Occasionally referring to the standards during planning and with students
- Checking to see if what is being taught can be found in the standards
- Beginning to understand the power and focus the standards provide and working to identify the essential understandings that are embedded in and that transcend the standards as they are written in the documents.
- Being able to truly say "I am standards-based because I used standards to design assessments and instruction and I used student work to judge whether or not instruction was well designed for this content with these learners."

Do you just reference the standards or are you truly a standards-based educator?

Reprinted from *Why Didn't I Learn This in College?*

In the middle school...

- Mr. Rugg visited Jessie Bliss' classroom and noted the active, hands-on learning taking place. Also apparent was the fact that classroom expectations had been established. Students were aware of the expectations and followed them.
- Laurie Rayhill, special education teacher, brought one of her students to Mr. Rugg's office at the beginning of this week. The student was not in trouble, but practiced giving an oral report in front of Mr. Rugg in preparation for giving her report to a classroom audience.
- Students in Mrs. Prodanovich's class watched a "Charlie Brown" video last week. The students were then asked to compare and contrast Linus and Charlie Brown. I was reminded of Mrs. Prodanovich's activity when reading the article "Invitations to Learn" by Carol Ann Tomlinson, in which she wrote, "The impetus to learn gradually does not come first from content itself, but rather because a teacher has learned to make the content inviting."

In the high school...

- A week of "mockery" in the high school! Students in the middle school and high school participated in the mock election conducted on Tuesday, November 5. This was the end activity of a unit that covered polling and the creation of brochures to educate "the public". Voter turnout was impressive (see results). Thanks to Kent Willmann and student teacher Anna Gardiner for organizing the mock election. What an excellent way for students to gain a deeper understanding of the political process.
- Hillary Jackson, student teacher in Mr. Lathrop's class, held a mock trial in English 11. The class read *Frankenstein* and the assignment was to try Dr. Frankenstein in a civil case that was brought forth by the "creation". Before "going to trial," the students had to learn about the court system and define terms such as malpractice, negligence, and emotional and physical distress. In preparation for the trial, students had to find quotes and passages from the book that supported their views. This activity incorporated reading comprehension skills and argumentative speaking.

Jessica Overboe, Silver Creek High School, St. Vrain Valley Public Schools, Longmont, CO

Peer Observation

Have you tried to implement a peer observation program, had early enthusiasm and then seen the program slowly fade away? This happens so often because it is difficult to add yet another event to an already busy school day. Yet we know that public teaching and conversations about shared professional experiences are extremely valuable to our professional growth.

Rather than starting with a full-fledged peer observation program, a good starting point for embedding peer observation into the life of the school is to start with **learning walks,** discussed on pages 37, and with school-wide initiatives like **Peer Poaching** and **Treasure Hunt**.

Peer Poaching

Dianna Lindsay, Headmaster at the Columbus Jewish Day School and former Principal of Worthington-Kilbourne High School, Columbus, Ohio, provided each staff member with three **peer poaching passes**. She explained to them that they were to visit three different classrooms to gather teaching ideas they might use. Upon leaving the classroom, they were to leave their passes on the teacher's desk. The teacher who was visited signed the pass and put it in a fish bowl in the front office. Once a month Dianna drew a pass out of the fish bowl to identify the monthly winners. She then provided them time to talk, plan, materials, or volunteered to teach their classes for a day.

Treasure Hunt

Bruce Oliver, Principal of Thoreau Middle School, Vienna, Virginia, had all faculty members draw the name of another faculty member out of a hat at a staff meeting. They were instructed to visit the classroom of the teacher whose name they had drawn and to complete an enlarged version of the form shown below. The forms were collected and posted on a bulletin board in the faculty lounge.

> ## Treasure Hunt
> **The treasure I found in** _____**'s classroom was:**

See Tool-14: Peer Poaching Pass

Peer Observation

Formalizing and Focusing the Peer Observation Process

Nancy Hurianek, Principal, and Sean Corey, Assistant Principal, at Prairie Ridge Elementary School in Longmont, Colorado, offer staff members the opportunity to participate in personal professional development through the peer observation process. The request and rationale form **(See Tool-13)** asks teachers to explain what they are hoping to learn and how it relates to the standards of learning, the school goals, and their own professional growth plans. Teachers are given the following guidelines.

Personal Professional Development Peer Observation Request

- Your classroom will be covered by either Nancy or Sean.
- You will need to provide the focus standards on which your students are working and the context for the instruction. (Where the students have been and where they are now in the learning process.) You do not need to provide specific lesson plans. We will take it from there.
- Complete the request and rationale form.
- Observation periods must be 45 minutes or less.
- Provide at least one week notice.

The above example involves no funds because the administrative staff covers the classes of the teachers who are peer observing. If funding is available, arrange for a regular substitute to be in the building for the sole purpose of supporting the peer observation program. It is a cost effective way to provide quality professional development for teachers.

Patrick Henry Elementary School Use of Substitute for Peer Observation

- SBE coaches observing teachers
- Teachers observing SBE coaches
- Teachers observing other teachers
- SBE coaches engaged in planning with teachers
- SBE coaches conferencing with teachers

2002-2003 school year: 72% of available substitute time used by staff.

See Tool-13: Peer Observation Request Form

Action Research

According to St. Vrain Valley School District's (Longmont, Colorado) **Results-Based Professional Development Models**, action research is:

- A methodical evaluation of topics or issues about teaching practice and student performance
- Research-based, data-driven, and centered on student learning
- A structure for determining areas of focus for research, for gathering data, and for writing summary reports that describe observations and findings
- Generates results that are talked about and shared with students and colleagues

For teachers who are both knowledgeable about and skilled in all areas of performance and who are by nature both reflective and analytical, action research provides an incredible opportunity for them to not only demonstrate their competency at an advanced level, but it is an appealing alternative to what may be for them meaningless classroom observations and written reports that offer little in the way of growth opportunities. While action research may be conducted by an individual teacher, the results should be shared with colleagues and impact their practice as well. A team approach to action research could provide valuable school improvement information and probably develop on-site expertise on the selected area of study. **The Results-Based Professional Development Models** cited above, as well as several **Tools for Schools** from the National Staff Development Council (NSDC) and a variety of books from the Association for Supervision and Evaluation (ASCD), provide in-depth information on the action research process.

MassPartners, a collaboration of seven professional associations in Massachusetts, includes in **Teaching Matters**, their position paper for the supervision and evaluation process, a recommendation that with the exception of novice teachers, all teachers engage in the **"development, implementation, and evaluation of a multiple-year professional development plan that includes examining student performance data."** The paper further suggests that teachers with more than four years experience in the district "work with one or more other teachers as partners, critical friends, or mentors in implementing the professional development plan." By using the formats presented in the sources mentioned earlier, these recommendations can be implemented as action research projects.

Getting Started with
Action Research

Consider

- If you are new to action research, start small! Don't choose anything too broad.
- If you are engaged in a school-wide or district-wide project, it may be a multi-year project. This type of project will require a strong commitment from the researchers and school leadership.

Possible Purposes of an Action Research Project

- to develop reflective, inquiry-based skills as a teaching professional
- to enhance teacher decision-making
- to pursue, in depth, a topic or research question that is important to you or your students
- to enhance student learning opportunities
- to transfer your discoveries to classroom practices

Selection of a Research Question or Topic

As you begin to come up with ideas or questions, you might want to ask yourself the following questions:

- What questions do I have about instruction either in a general sense or in the context of my own teaching? (Example: How should phonics be incorporated in instruction? How should I teach spelling? When/How should I group for math instruction?)
- What issues have I been wrestling with as a teacher?
- What teaching methods would I like to investigate more fully in an action research study?
- What topics interest me most?
- Based on student data, what do I/we need to know or learn?

Some of the most valuable classroom research begins with small questions, with the wonderings of individual teachers as they engage in day-to-day work with their students.

Data Collection Possibilities

We are surrounded by data. We simply need to get over being defensive about it and use it to inform our practice. This list provides a starting point for thinking about the data that is, or could easily be, available to us.

- Pre/post test scores
- Attendance reports
- Grade distribution sheets
  - Across departments
  - Across teachers
  - Across schools
  - Longitudinal
- Standardized test results
- Student portfolios
  - Across students
  - Same students across time
- Student work
  - Across the same assignments
  - Across grade levels
  - Across schools
  - Across teachers
  - Using rubrics
- Field notes
- Audiotapes
- Chart patterns over time
- Videos
- Student journals
- Interviews
- Questionnaires
- Surveys
- Review of the literature
- Document analysis
  - Provides perspective
  - Provides context and background
- Case studies
- Chart patterns over time

Getting Started with Action Research
Important Questions to Consider

Issue
- What is the focus of your action research?
- Why is this an important challenge or issue?
- What needs to be understood or developed?
- How will learning more about this issue contribute to improved learning for students?

Guiding Questions or Hypothesis
- What do you know already?
- What does research or a review of the literature tell you?
- What question or hypothesis will guide your research?

Methods and Procedures
- What will you do to answer the question?
- How will you do the research and what resources will be used?

Data Gathering and Reporting
- What data will you gather?
- How might that data answer your question?
- How can you ensure that data gathering methods are replicable?
- How can you use multiple sources of data?
- How will you include multiple perspectives?

Data Analysis
- What does the analysis of the data reveal?
- What patterns or trends did you discover?
- What relationships did you see between data?

Action Planning Implications and Significance
- What have you learned and what will you do as a result?

Reporting Results
- What new questions emerged as a result of your study?
- What documentation will you include with your report?
- How will the results be shared with colleagues?

Adapted from Results-Based Professional Development Models, St. Vrain Valley School District, Longmont, CO

Looking at Assignments and Student Work

Much is being written about ways to productively look at student work in collaborative settings. When teachers engage in these processes, it makes a great deal of sense for the principal to sit in on the meetings. Several of the protocols or processes currently in use are described below.

Education Trust

Education Trust created a process that helps teachers align classroom work with standards. The scoring tool is used to focus participants on the quality of classroom assignments and their direct connection with standards. Use of this approach can help teachers design rigorous assignments. Analysis of student products helps identify adjustments needed in the assignment directions and levels of teacher support needed to ensure student success.

Education Trust's Standards in Practice

- The teacher presenting the assignment explains how and when the assignment was given and what the students were expected to learn as a result of completing the assignment. The presenting teacher also spends a few minutes working through the problem or explaining what the response should look like.

- The collaborative group asks questions about the assignment. They in essence do a task analysis of what students would have to know and be able to do to successfully complete the assignment.

- Next the group identifies the standards, benchmarks, and level of thinking required by the task using Bloom's Taxonomy.

- The team then generates a rubric or other scoring tool to describe successful completion of the assignment.

- The teacher presents student work from the assignment and the team scores the work using the scoring tool they have generated.

- After the scoring, the group discusses possible revisions to the assignment and what to do about students who did not demonstrate competency with the standards the assignment addressed.

The last step in the Education Trust process is quite different from traditional practice around the data obtained from student work. In the past the norm was to simply record the number correct or the grade in the grade book and move on. While planning standards-based instruction is a challenge in and of itself, revision of instruction and assignments as a result of the analysis of student work requires a completely new way of thinking and working. Discussions about the significance of this shift provide learning opportunities for both teachers and administrators.

Looking at Assignments and Student Work

Project Zero

Steve Seidel and his colleagues at Harvard's Project Zero created a process that provides opportunities for teachers to examine and discuss pieces of student work in structured conversation with their peers, coaches, and supervisors.

Project Zero's Collaborative Assessment Conference

Getting Started: The presenting teacher or team shares copies of the selected student work, without making comments about the work or the assignment.

Describing the work: The other participants examine the work and describe what they notice without making any judgments about the quality of the work or their personal preferences.

Raising questions: They then pose questions about the student, the assignment, the curriculum, or any other area. The teacher/team members take notes but do not respond.

Speculating about what standards are the focus of the student work: The participants "guess" what the child was working on when he/she created the piece. This could include the standards, benchmarks, and indicators on which the student was focused or the skills the child was trying to master, questions the child was trying to answer, or ideas he/she was trying to express.

Teacher response: The teacher or team responds to the comments made in the review process. She/they provide information to clarify intent and contextual background, engage in reflective discussion with the reviewers and ask their own questions.

Closing the Conference: The group reflects on their learning and the process. The presenting teacher's efforts and presentation are acknowledged.

The implications of this process for teaching, learning and leading are tremendous. Attention and energy is appropriately focused on the work of students and of the school. It does, however, require that there be a high level of trust in the competence and benevolence of all participants and that the presenting teacher or team of teachers not be defensive about data, data analysis and questioning.

Resources for Looking at Student Work

- www.lasw.org (lasw = looking at student work.) This website features the collaborative assessment conference and provides multiple links to related websites.
- www.annenberginstitute.org/publications

Looking at Assignments and Student Work

Writing Rubrics Using Student Work

This process is a productive way to engage staff in collegial discussions about student work and to establish consistency across teachers about what work does and does not meet the standards of performance established by the school community. As the educational leader, you can either facilitate or participate in these discussions and at the same time gather data about the thinking of teachers about what excellent work looks like. These discussions help staff meet school goals of consistently clear and high expectations, provide the opportunity for informal professional development for staff, and the teaching staff leaves the meeting with rubrics ready for classroom use.

The Process

- Sort the work in to broad categories: **excellent, okay,** and **needs work**.
- Identify two or three strong examples of each category.
- Start with the **excellent** examples and list the attributes that make them excellent.
- Continue the process with the **okay** and **needs work** examples.
- Write these attributes into a holistic rubric.
- Be sure that an attribute listed in any one category is also listed in the other two. If you want to turn your holistic rubric into an analytical rubric, sort by attributes and assign a rating to each of the attributes.

Getting Started

The ninth grade English team at West Springfield High School, Springfield, Virginia, developed a rubric to assess student writing. On Thursdays they have a brown bag lunch and score the work of each other's students using the rubric they designed.

Teachers in Churchville-Chili School District, Churchville, New York, examined second grade student work using a district-wide writing rubric. A collection of student writing samples from September, November, January, and March were scored and the ratings recorded in a different color for each month. This enabled them to see growth over time and to pose questions as to what the data told them and to design next steps in working with those students.

Looking at Assignments and Student

Data Driven Decision Teams (3-D Teams)

In an effort to use data to make solid instructional decisions, groups of teachers meet once or twice a month to review and analyze student work. The analysis, reflection, and collegial collaboration provides a framework for decision making about future instruction. This practice is a particularly useful tool for teachers who are striving for consistency across classrooms in a standards-based learning and assessment environment.

The group members bring samples of student work to the meeting. Hanson, Silver and Strong, in descriptions of their Authentic Achievement Teams, suggest that each teacher bring six pieces of students' work to the meeting; they further recommend that the samples represent different achievement levels or different levels of success on this particular assignment. For example, two might be from the top third of a class, two from the middle, and two from the bottom. An alternative approach would be to **analyze the work of "regular" students and that of second language learners, advanced learners, or inclusion students.** It is also helpful to bring copies of any directions given to the students.

If the group members have not planned together, ten to fifteen minutes is spent looking through the student work samples and any teacher artifacts so that all participants get a good idea of what kind of work they will be discussing and analyzing.

The participants can agree to analyze all the work of their students around the same set of criteria, or each teacher can indicate the questions, concerns, and criteria to be considered for that set of student work. In either case, the outcomes of the discussion might be directed toward:

- checking for **validation** about the appropriateness of the work for the developmental stage of the students
- checking to ensure that the task is **congruent** with the stated mastery objective and/or state or district standards
- checking for **consistency** of opinion about the assessment and evaluation of the work
- possible **adjustments** in teacher directions and **support** for all/some of the students

1st Grade Third Trimester Action Plan

School Goal: 60-63% of students will be reading at or above grade level

Student Names	Student Data	Instructional Goals	Strategies, Action, Resources and Evidence
Ariel Derek Jordan Kai Luis Michael Marisa Nathaniel Paul Sean Vanessa	• Students still scoring at 2-3 level on Retelling Rubric (proficient basic/proficient) • Focus: Verbal expression of ideas without prompting	Retell a story in logical, sequential order - including beginning, middle, and end (using the words first, then, next, last) Also, students will give details while recalling events.	• Model through read-aloud; think-aloud • Continued opportunities to retell stories • Take-home reading comprehension activities • Writing and sequencing activities • Evaluation=Retelling Rubric ▲ Work samples/completed activities

Alyssa
Chan
Chris
Tam
William
	• Reading/recognizing words at .50 level
	• Goal: reading at .50-.75 fluently
		Read at least 75 grade level words from Reading Words assessment, and demonstrate understanding of text by using words in sentences and discussing words read.	• "Right Start Reading" methods - small group/individualized instruction
			• Phonological tasks
			• Evaluation=Theme tests
			  ▲ Vocabulary Checklists
			  ▲ Spelling Sentences
			  ▲ Informal R.R.

Don
Kelly
Sarah
	• Reading/recognizing words at .25 level
	• Identifying beginning sounds - "slide to the end of the word" (sound blending)
	• Identifying when words/phrases do not make sense
		Recognize all lowercase and uppercase letters, and demonstrate phonemic awareness. Read at least 26 grade level words from Reading Words assessment and demonstrate understanding of text	• Word Wall activities
			  ➤ Daily review
			  ➤ Weekly word checklists
			• Spelling/writing/daily oral language

Loma Linda Elementary School, St. Vrain Valley School District, Longmont, CO

Looking at Student Work in the Classroom

I want to assist you in further implementation of a standards-based classroom. Please know that I am going to spend at least as much time looking for evidence of student learning as I am observing your teaching. Listed below are certain indicators that I will be looking for during observations:

- There is evidence that standards/essential questions and tasks are the focus of what you are teaching and what students are learning. For example, your lesson plan might reflect the content standards/essential questions and tasks on which you and the students are focused.
- Students are able to explain the relationship between the current lesson or activity and the standards/essential questions and tasks.
- Students are given opportunities to practice and improve their performance in a variety of ways. That is, differentiated instruction is used to meet various learning styles and needs .
- Assessment results are used to guide instruction.
- Students know what is expected, in advance, where they stand in relation to the performance level expected, and what they can do to improve.
- A variety of assessments is used to provide evidence of student proficiency.
- There is evidence that students are asking good questions and self-assessing their own work against performance criteria.
- Questions that prompt students to be critical thinkers and evaluators are used.
- Students are actively engaged in their tasks and clearly understand it is their obligation to perform and learn.

Questions I might pose to students during observations:

- What are you learning?
- How are you doing in this class?
- How do you know when you are doing well?
- How is what you are doing helping you learn?
- Can you share with me something you have learned?

Erica Bowman, Principal of Mountain View Elementary School in Longmont, Colorado, includes this document in the packet of materials she gives teachers. It clearly articulates and communicates what she would be looking for and what she will be asking students about during both formal and informal observations. She shared this as an artifact in her presentation on how she was using information from professional development opportunities provided to new principals.

Coaching and Mentoring for ALL

Everyone should always have a mentor and always be a mentor. We all know the old saying, **"Even champions need coaches!"** New administrators, even superintendents, need coaches and mentors. It stands to reason that novice teachers need really outstanding and committed mentors. If we have not had practice mentoring and/or collaborating with each other on an ongoing basis, mentoring relationships in an organized induction program can feel contrived and be quite superficial.

It is important to pay attention to the context into which a induction program is introduced. If the induction process is seen as an event rather than a way of being, then only novice teachers will be "inducted" and this induction will be a series of events and interactions to be marked off on a checklist. The process will be defined by a new teacher orientation in the late summer and the assignment of a mentor whose appointment absolves the rest of the staff from any responsibility for the success of new staff members.

If, however, the induction program is a part of a school where all staff members are committed to the success of all other staff members, then the arrival of new staff to the school, to the team, to the department, and even the arrival of new administrators is handled quite differently. **If it is the norm for all to mentor and all to seek a mentor, the interactions play out in quite different ways.**

If you want or need to design or refine your induction program, it is important to not only attend to the context into which the program will be introduced, it is essential to identify the outcomes you want to obtain as a result of the induction program before planning any events or identifying who will be mentors.

The most important, and perhaps the only necessary, outcome to include is **"A fully qualified and satisfied teacher in each classroom."** This outcome is appropriate because we want a fully qualified teacher in each classroom. Given the projected need for over two million new teachers in the next decade as well as the time, energy, and expense of ensuring that our new hires are fully qualified, we also want them to be fully satisfied so that they continue to teach in the district. Your definition of fully qualified should come from your district standards and criteria included in your teacher performance review documents.

Keep your eye on the goal... Student learning facilitated by a fully qualified and satisfied teacher in every classroom!

We Are All On The Same Team!
Roles and Responsibilities in Induction Programs

In a well established multi-year induction program all district personnel have multiple roles to plan in ensuring that there is a fully qualified and satisfied teacher in each classroom. The following list lays out some of the essential roles and responsibilities of staff members.

All Members of the School District Staff

- Ensure a strong start to the school year by providing time, resources, and support to novice teachers even before the opening of school. The superintendent, district office staff, and school based staff to include the administration, the teaching staff, the clerical staff, and the custodial staff should all play a role.
- Provide information and support. Do not ask, "Do you need anything?" Instead identify what new staff members are most likely to need in:
  - Instructional support
  - Professional support
  - Personal support
  - Logistical support
        ... and provide it!

The District Office Staff

to include the superintendent, curriculum, and instruction office, professional development office, and human resources

- Inform new hires of district expectations not only around contractual obligations, but around teaching practices and professional interactions
- Provide copies of appropriate curriculum documents
- Provide copies of new teacher resources like *Why Didn't I Learn This in College?*
- Provide professional development opportunities designed to meet the needs of novice teachers and those new to the district

The Principal

- Provides working conditions for the novice teacher that facilitate success: minimize special programs, moving from room to room, multiple preparations
- Organizes the school environment so that collaboration is more easily accomplished, meeting time is focused on instruction, where instructional decision making and student work is made public, clearly articulate expectations that all staff members are to be supportive of new teaching staff in both professional and personal ways.

We Are All On The Same Team!
Roles and Responsibilities in Induction

- Identify mentors using criteria established by the district
- Facilitate interaction between mentors and novice teachers by providing release time for them to plan, reflect, and observe together

School Staff
- Department chairs and/or team leaders share unit and lesson plans, as well as unwritten customs and norms of behavior, and provide "big picture" of how the department or team functions
- All staff members make resources readily available and work to articulate rationales for actions, directions, or requests
- Front office staff and custodial staff explicitly offer assistance in obtaining and/or adjusting resources

Mentors
- Serve as an advocate
- Serve as a resource
- Maintain a confidential relationship with the novice teacher
- Provide a variety of perspectives rather than only own perspective
- Serve as the "go-to" person

Novice Teachers
- Seek out help
- Observe other teachers teaching, planning, reflecting, and conferencing
- Ask why things are done the way they are
- Participate in professional development opportunities
- Demonstrate a willingness to watch, listen, and learn
- Share own expertise gained from recent university and student experiences

Experienced Teachers New to District, School, Team, or Department
- Seek out help
- Demonstrate a willingness to watch, listen, and learn
- Observe other teachers teaching, planning, reflecting, and conferencing
- Ask why things are done the way they are
- Diplomatically share past experiences that can help inform practice in this new setting
- Participate in professional development opportunities

Mentor-Novice Teacher Interactions

Types of Interactions:
- Meeting/conference with novice teacher
- Visit novice teacher during instructional time (informal or formal observation)
- Telephone/email conversation with novice teacher
- Joint observation of another teacher by mentor and novice teacher
- Network with other mentors
- Demonstrate lesson for novice teacher
- Dialogue journals

Frequency of Interactions:
- The frequency of interactions will depend on the needs of the novice teacher. These guidelines are suggested as minimums for interacting with the novice teacher.
  - As much as possible before school starts
  - Once a day during the first month of school
  - Two to three times a week the rest of first semester
  - At least once a week throughout the second semester
- Experienced teachers new to the district, as well as second and third year teachers, need continued support and should have the opportunity to interact purposefully with a mentor or a mentor support team at least twice a month.

Communication Possibilities
- Face-to-face interactions to include conversations, conferences, planning sessions, co-observations, and socialization
- Emails
- Telephone conversations
- Notes
- Dialogue journals

Possible Activities:
- Assist in obtaining appropriate materials, equipment, and furniture and in setting up the classroom before school starts
- Review district standards, benchmarks, and indicators
- Conduct overview of curriculum and main curriculum materials
- Explain how you plan for the year, the unit, and the lesson
- Jointly plan instruction
- Jointly design resource materials
- Jointly plan parent conferences
- Jointly conduct parent conferences

Mentor-Novice Teacher Interactions

Possible Activities continued:

- Analyze and assess the novice teacher's practice in relation to the district's teacher performance criteria
- Explain supervision and evaluation process
- Practice report card procedures
- Share catalogs for ordering materials and equipment
- Share lessons and units that have been field tested by you or your colleagues
- Brainstorm a list of possible solutions to common organizational problems
- Explain your own and others' record keeping systems

District Documents to Structure Mentoring Work:

- State and District Standards, Benchmarks, and Indicators
- Curriculum Guides
- School Improvement Plan
- Professional Development Catalog
- Teacher Evaluation Performance Criteria
- School and district handbooks
- Staff and student directories
- School district calendar

Experienced teachers new to the district, grade level, department or team need mentors too. Use the above recommendations or create your own using only the headings. No matter how many years military or foreign service personnel have accumulated in their careers they are assigned a "sponsor" when they arrive at a new post overseas. The sponsor is responsible for making them feel welcome, introducing them to their friends and others they need to know, providing them what they need to live until their own goods arrive, and explaining the "way things are done around here." We in education should do no less!

Building Collaborative Teams

Collaboration is Not Optional!

In schools where collaborative cultures and professional learning communities are the norm, everyone is expected to be on a team or teams. It may be a grade level team, a vertical team, a school improvement team, or a curriculum development team. Unfortunately, these teams are not always as productive as they might be. The reasons that many teams are ineffective, or even dysfunctional, include the lack of clearly articulated and agreed upon goals or that team members lack the communication and collaboration skills for working together in the interest of student learning.

The study of **school culture** is important because it, as well as **individual belief systems** of team members, will have direct bearing on team effectiveness and team activities at each school.

Because team development does not happen quickly or in a linear fashion, team members need to understand the **change process**.

Team members must become experts in planning, leading, and participating in effective meetings.

Team members should complement each other; that is, they should learn to recognize, seek out, appreciate, and capitalize on **differences in styles, skills, talents, and interests**.

Teams need to constantly assess and work to improve **communication** within teams and with those "outside" the team.

Teams, early in the development process, should put in place **systems for dealing with problems and conflicts** and for making necessary adjustments in plans and procedures.

Team success depends on the degree to which members needs for **influence and parity** as well as a **sense of competence and confidence** are met.

Team members must **take the initiative** to share ideas and practices they value and believe will strengthen their efforts. They must also be willing to **give up some autonomy** to accomplish actions based on common visions and agreements.

The high levels of commitment, energy, and enthusiasm typical at the beginning of the teaming experience can be maintained only with **reflective practice, a balance of autonomy and interdependence, guidance, training, and support**.

Long-Term
Multifaceted Professional Development
including building in-house capacity

Do You Hear What We Hear?

We hear...performance assessment, differentiation, inclusion, block scheduling, rubrics, time and learning, direct instruction, constructivism, brain-compatible classrooms, reading in the content areas, instructional technology, thinking as a basic skill, balanced literacy, and on and on and on! All of these are important components of an instructional repertoire. The dilemma is that we try to implement them one by one, often a new one each year, rather than identifying patterns and integrating them thoughtfully, over long periods of time, into our work.

We also hear of schools and school districts offering a **potpourri of professional development opportunities** that are half-day or one day on a topic with no follow-up other than another professional development opportunity on yet another topic often facilitated by someone who has no clue what happened at the last sessions. **This does not work!** Such events do not change decision making and professional practice, so there is no improvement in student achievement. Yet we continue to use this model. Anyone interested in providing professional development that makes a difference should consult the **National Staff Development's Standards for Professional Development** for guidance. Another source of guidance is to examine the practices of the schools and school district that have received the **U.S. Department of Education's award for Model Professional Development.**

Focus! Focus! Focus!

Student learning is the goal! The **RPLIM Model** that originated with Fred Wood from the University of Oklahoma provides guidelines for establishing a focused and sustained professional development program. The acronym stands for **Readiness, Planning, Learning, Implementation, and Maintenance.** See the **Appendices** for St. Vrain Valley School District's brochure titled RPLIM Model for Results-Based Professional Development.

The following pages chronicle two school districts long-term, multifaceted professional development initiatives. Each includes building in-house capacity and job-embedded learning, in addition to workshops led by internal and external presenters.

A Long-Term Multifaceted Professional Development Plan

The following is an overview of the Induction and Training Program for Standards-Based Education at the Middle School Level, Martin Middle School, Taunton School District, Taunton, MA. All in-district professional development opportunities were organized and led by J. Henderson and A. Malmquist who participated in Leading the Learning and Job Embedded Learning in school years 1999-2000 and 2000-2001.

School Year 1999-2000
Leading the Learning
Mass Insight Education
ASK Group Consultant Deb Reed

Summer 2000
Intensive SBE Workshop
A 40-hour training

School Year 2000-2001
Job-Embedded Learning
Mass Insight Education
ASK Group Consultant Louise Thompson

Leading the Learning
Mass Insight Education
ASK Group Consultant Deb Reed

Fall 2000
Overview of Standards-Based Education
A presentation at the October district professional day training

Spring 2001
Overview of SBE and Critical Questions
A 40-hour after school focus group

Development of SBE Units
A 40-hour after school focus group

Where are We Going with SBE
A March district professional day program

June 2001
School Committee approved funding for Standards-Based 8th grade team

A Long-Term Multifaceted Professional Development Plan

Continued overview of the Induction and Training Program for Standards-Based Education at the Middle School Level, Martin Middle School, Taunton School District, Taunton, MA. All in-district professional development opportunities were organized and led by J. Henderson and A. Malmquist who participated in Leading the Learning and Job-Embedded Learning in school years 1999-2000 and 2000-2001.

Summer 2001 **Planning SBE Units and Interdisciplinary Units**
A 120-hour focus group over the summer

Fall 2001 **Planning Interdisciplinary Units: Advanced SBE Training**
October district professional day training

Fall-Spring 2001-2002 **Planning SBE Units**
A focus group for teachers to develop SBE units

Spring 2002 **Planning SBE Units and Interdisciplinary Units**
The March district Professional day

Spring 2002 **Ed Reform and the Standards-Based Classroom**

Future Plans
- Summer focus groups to continue to develop units
- Input all units onto school website for universal use
- Develop more interdisciplinary grade level teams
- Begin working on essential questions as a district/community

A Long-Term Multifaceted Professional Development Plan

The following is an overview of ASK Group work with Alexandria City Public Schools (ACPS), Alexandria, Virginia, on the SBE teacher leader cadre initiative, the induction program, leadership training, and building in-house capacity:

April 12, 1999	Standards of Learning planning meeting
April 26, 1999	Teacher Leader Cadre Members identified*
August 1999	Four days of training for teacher leaders
	Each teacher in ACPS provided a copy of *Instruction for All Students*
October 1999 - March 2000	Five training sessions for teacher leaders
November 1999 - May 2000	Leading the Learning workshop: Six days of training for all administrators
February - April 2000	Five days of classroom observations by consultant and administrators
April 2000	Meeting with leaders to discuss alignment of supervision and evaluation process with SBE
August 14 - 17, 2000	Four days of training for secondary teacher leaders*
August 2002	All teachers new to ACPS provided a copy of *Instruction for All Students*
September 2000 - March 2001	Three days of training for elementary teacher leaders*
September 2000 - May 2001	Twenty days of training and coaching for administrators/leadership staff
September 2001	All new teachers provided a copy of *Instruction for All Students*
September 2001 - May 2002	Four days of training for administrators/leadership staff
	Two workshops for Minnie Howard staff on differentiation
	Two workshops on instructional strategies for STEP, the alternative high school staff
	Four days of training for teacher leader cadre

*As an outcome of their training, teacher leaders planned and facilitated five to six days of site-based professional development during school years 1999-2000 and 2000-2001. During school year 2001-2002, their roles varied from building to building.

**Training, consulting, and facilitation provided by ASK Group members Fran Prolman, Paula Rutherford and Elizabeth Rossini.

Continued overview of ASK Group work with Alexandria City Public Schools (ACPS), Alexandria, Virginia, on the SBE teacher leader cadre initiative, the induction program, leadership training, and building in-house capacity:

July 2002	Three days of training for mentor teachers
September 2002 - May 2003	Work with SBE Team at Patrick Henry Elementary School as they add collegial coaching around classroom observations and walk throughs to their repertoire
September 2003	All new teachers given copies of *Why Didn't I Learn This in College?* and *Instruction for All Students*
October 2002	Mentor support meeting
November 2002 - May 2003	Two site visits to each mentor to provide support for their work with novice teachers
November 2002	Workshop on Active Learning Strategies for elementary and secondary teachers
	Workshop on Creating a Learning-Center Classroom for elementary and secondary teachers
December 2002	Leadership staff workshop on using *Why Didn't I Learn This in College?* as a job-embedded professional development tool
January 2003	Leadership staff workshop on using *Instruction for All Students* as a job-embedded professional development tool
	Mentor support meeting to plan for reflective work around first semester, guidelines for observations and/or co-observations and guidance in using *Why Didn't I Learn This in College?* with novice teachers
March 2003	Mentor support meeting
May 2003	Mentor and novice teacher celebration!
July 2003	*Why Didn't I Learn This in College?* Summer Institute for new teachers
	Mentors and lead mentors for 2003-2004 selected
August 2003	Mentor and lead mentor training for 2003-2004
	Mentors work with novice teachers and teachers new to the district teachers during orientation week
September 2003 - May 2004	Quarterly support meetings for mentors
	Quarterly support meetings for new teachers
	Two support site visits to each mentor

History of
Supervision and Evaluation

Our Past

Each educational leader has a unique history with the supervision and evaluation processes used in school districts across the land. Few have found that the process, as implemented with them as teachers, had much impact on their practice. Given that, when those same teachers move into administrative roles, they place little to no value on the process. Instead, most see it as something that has to be completed as a contractual requirement. There are not many educational leaders who use the supervision and evaluation process as a professional development opportunity. Given their past experiences with the process, this is not surprising.

The most frequently used supervision and evaluation process is the **clinical supervision** process. This process includes a pre-conference, an observation of classroom instruction, the analysis and interpretation of the observation, written observation report, and a post conference. While there are multiple approaches to use in planning and conducting the conferences that follow observations, the approach most often used is for the supervisor/evaluator to summarize the lesson, make commendations, and give suggestions, recommendations, or directives. Most administrators keep a log so they can check off completion of each component of the progress and find themselves late at night sitting at their computers writing the observation reports. The supervisor is doing all the work of analyzing the lesson and the teacher is waiting to hear and read whether or not the supervisor liked what he or she saw. Thomas Sergiovanni calls this process a **non-event** because so little comes from it. This process, well executed, is an important part of our supervisory repertoire and an essential one for documenting teachers who are ineffective, but it is only one alternative. Thank goodness peer coaches, critical friends, and mentors have shown us alternative ways of discussing teaching and learning in ways that promote teacher growth and student learning.

It is time to stop moving through the process on automatic pilot. It is both too time consuming and too rich an opportunity to have the process not be embedded in the everyday life of school. It also needs to be an important part of the data we use to inform our decisions about how to spend our time, our energy, and our resources. On the previous pages, a wide array of collegial interactions and leadership roles for all educators has been discussed. Each of these can be, and should be, included in the supervision and evaluation process of all educators.

The Present

The standards movement, with its emphasis on clearly articulated learning goals for all students, has had a huge impact on the move to provide clarification and articulation of performance indicators for educators. Most states, as well as several organizations such as the **National Board of Professional Teaching Standards** and the **Council of Chief State School Officers,** have identified areas of performance and, to varying degrees of specificity, indicators of performance for teachers and administrators.

That is the good news. The bad news is that, in the moment, implementation of supervision and evaluation processes in the interest of teacher growth and student learning is all over the map. While clearly articulating performance indicators is a big step in the right direction, that alone is not sufficient to ensure the supervision and evaluation process becomes an integral part of our professional lives in a way that honors the knowledge and skills of most teachers. This process parallels the stages teachers move through in becoming standards-based educators. (see pages 172-175 in *Why Didn't I Learn This in College?*).

Many teachers and most administrators spend a significant amount of time in the "standards/criteria-referenced" stage of development before identifying the essential understandings and the key concepts on which to focus and before developing a clear picture of what it looks like when the learners/teachers have met with success. If we are not careful, the newly designed indicators can become yet another checklist opportunity.

The

Future

2000s

1990s

1980s

1970s

1960s

1950s

The "REAL" Dark Ages

History of Supervision and Evaluation

1st
What do we want our supervision and evaluation process to accomplish?

2nd
What data do we need to know we've accomplished what we want to accomplish?

3rd
What do we need to do to get there?

What Does The Future Hold?

It all depends. We can continue to implement supervision and evaluation processes in ways that meet contractual obligations or we can seize the moment and use what we are learning through the implementation of standards-based education to enhance the learning opportunities of adults. We can do this by identifying different goals for our supervisory efforts and then implementing the process in ways designed to get to that new end. Some of the variables to consider are:

- A New Mental Model for Supervision and Evaluation
- Aligning the Processes
- Clearly Articulated Standards and Professional Development for Leaders
- The ASK Construct
- Professional Development for All
- The Power of Conversations
- Differentiated Supervision

A New Mental Model

Two school districts navigating the choppy waters of recreating their supervision and evaluation processes, using the new mental model suggested by WestED in **Standards: From Document to Dialogue**, are Barrington School District #220 in Barrington, Illinois and St. Vrain Valley School District in Longmont, Colorado. Both districts are focusing their work on student learning, creating professional learning communities, and making data driven decisions.

Each district began the process of revising its supervision and evaluation process by engaging staff in discussions about the possibility of having the process be more than it was in its current form. Focus groups and teams said with strong voices that the time expended in the supervision and evaluation process was not well spent, that the time spent writing the observation reports decreased opportunities for conversations about teaching and learning, and that the process seemed separate from everything else going on in the system.

The Future of
Supervision and Evaluation

After establishing the purposes and desired outcomes of the process, the next step was asking what they wanted students to know and be able to do, not around specific content but around how they would be as consumers and producers of knowledge. With those student outcomes identified, they then asked what would teachers need to know and do to lead students to those outcomes. Then, and only then, did the district committees identify criteria aligned with the desired student outcomes. These questions of what do we want our supervision and evaluation systems to accomplish, what data would we need to know if that was happening, and what action plans do we need around data gathering, analysis, and feedback options followed the SBE Planning Process.

The graphic below represents the four components each district considered in the revision of the supervision and evaluation process.

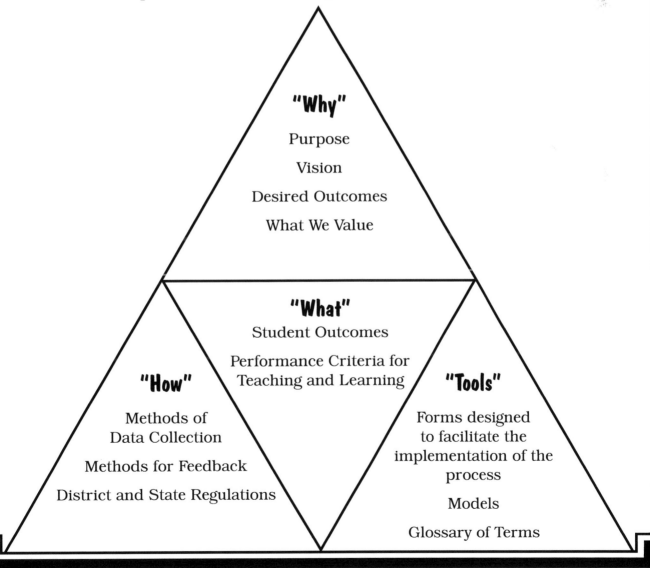

"Why"

Purpose

Vision

Desired Outcomes

What We Value

"What"

Student Outcomes

Performance Criteria for
Teaching and Learning

"How"

Methods of
Data Collection

Methods for Feedback

District and State Regulations

"Tools"

Forms designed
to facilitate the
implementation of the
process

Models

Glossary of Terms

Excerpts from
The Vision Statement
for the Supervision and Evaluation Process
Poudre School District, Ft. Collins, Colorado

Just as we nurture and promote the growth of our students, so too do we affirm and support our own professional growth through the evaluation process. Good faith and trust between professionals and empowerment of each individual to reach the heights that they have chosen will foster the positive growth-supporting system needed.

This system is based on good teaching practices and is not a child of any particular educational methodology.

A partnership between principals and teachers to support growth is a new concept, which will eventually generate a radical new relationship. Elements of this new relationship include joint/active participation and shared responsibility for improvement between evaluator and evaluatee. We expect growth to be promoted by comments citing commendations and recommendations which empower teachers and principals. This continuous cooperative nature was first imagined and then developed through the joint efforts of a committee of teachers selected by the Poudre Education Association and administrators. Through our struggles, we have sensed the tremendous power for good this system promises. We hope that the strength and knowledge we have gained by learning about evaluation will one day translate into the same growth and empowerment for all Poudre School District teachers and principals.

Beliefs
- The process of evaluation shall be continuous and cooperative.
- The most effective evaluation occurs when teachers are empowered to self-evaluate.
- The improvement of instruction is a responsibility shared by both the evaluator and the evaluatee.
- The interaction between the teacher and the students is a key factor in the instructional process and shall be emphasized in the evaluation process.
- The written evaluation form shall include both commendations on a teacher's strength and plans for continued growth.
- The evaluation shall be used when making administrative decisions concerning recommendations for re-employment, continuing employment, transfer, promotion, or discipline.
- Each individual is included in the planning and responsibility for his/her own professional growth.

The Future
Supervision and Evaluation

1st
What do we want our supervision and evaluation process to accomplish?

2nd
What data do we need to know we've accomplished what we want to accomplish?

3rd
What do we need to do to get there?

Aligning the Processes

In order to make the supervision and evaluation process more than an event to be checked off as completed, it must be aligned with other district Processes and must be a part of ongoing conversations and communications throughout the school year. Just as the message of the mission and vision statements of the district must be reflected in the data gathering, analysis, and feedback processes, as well as in the criteria for professional performance, the language of the supervision and evaluation documents should be used in these processes:

- Hiring and interviewing process
- Induction program
- Professional development needs assessments
- Professional development at the district, school, and team levels
- Faculty, department, and team meetings
- Professional growth plans
- School improvement plans

Clearly Articulated Standards of Performance and Professional Development for School Leaders

It is essential that school leaders be provided direction and support for implementing supervision and evaluation processes in new ways. Many current school leaders have not taught in a standards-based classroom, so they need extensive information and practice in understanding, modeling, noticing, and analyzing teaching and learning in a standards-based environment. While high quality professional development is essential, it is in those districts where the district leadership holds school administrators accountable for their work as instructional leaders that student achievement increases. West Irondequoit Central School District in Rochester, New York, is a prime example of a district that has provided consistent focused professional development opportunities for school leaders, holds them accountable for using the supervision and evaluation process as learning opportunities, and for making data driven decisions. Student achievement data consistently reflects this intense focus on learning accountability for all.

The Future of
Supervision and Evaluation

Many districts do not have published criteria for school administrators. It is time for all districts to do so. The Council of Chief State School Officers published Standards for School Leaders in 1996. This document provides an excellent starting point for the design of school district standards for school leaders. The document can be accessed at www.ccsso.org as the **Interstate School Leaders Licensure Consortium: Standards for School Leaders.**

The ASK Construct

Our **attitudes, skills, and knowledge (ASK)** influence every decision we make. Individually, or in combination, they cause us to place a high priority on one task and to procrastinate about another. Sometimes we know something, but are not skilled at using that knowledge in appropriate or productive ways. Sometimes we are both knowledgeable and skilled, but our attitudes about the situation cause us to avoid action. Both teachers and leaders need to self-assess around their own attitudes, skills, and knowledge and then learn to analyze the decision making and actions of others through the same lens.

For educators there are three components embedded in each of the three variables, **A S K**. That is, educators must consider their **KNOWLEDGE about content, about learners and learning theory, and about repertoire for connecting the learners, and the content**. Lack of knowledge about one of more of those components can cause problems. Even when one has knowledge about content, learners and learning theory, and has a rich repertoire of instructional strategies, issues surface if there is a lack of **SKILL** in applying that knowledge in a given situation. For instance, a teacher could have considerable knowledge of and skills with the curriculum at the fifth grade level and really enjoy, understand and work well with fifth graders. When that teacher is assigned to teach second grade he may have to revise or develop a new repertoire of strategies for working with students of that age and may struggle with chunking the content in ways so that it is accessible to second graders. The response to a new assignment may sound like an **ATTITUDE** problem when, in fact, it is an expression of fear caused by concerns about a lack of knowledge and skill to be successful in a new situation. Consequently, supervisors, coaches, and mentors need to develop skills at uncovering the real issues. The more closely we identify whether an issue is rooted in knowledge, skills, or attitudes, the better we can plan our interactions.

See **Tool-21: Data Analysis Using ASK Contstruct** and **Tool-25: ASK Goal Setting.**

The Future of
Supervision and Evaluation

Trust and Rapport

Relationships are key. This is not a reference to congeniality. It is a reference to a belief in the benevolence and competence of the professionals with whom we are working. Trust is a two way street. Supervisors and mentors have to believe, until proven wrong, in the benevolence and quest for competence of the teachers with whom they work. Conversely, the teachers have to believe in the benevolence and competence of those who supervise them. Without such trust a great deal of energy is spent trying to figure out the motivation of the other party, and ways to avoid working collaboratively with that person. If either party engages in a **gotcha** mentality, then the effects of any efforts are minimized. Unfortunately, there prevails in many schools a **we-they** mentality instead of a culture built on mutual respect and an acceptance, even an embrace of, differentiated responsibilities in the interest of student learning.

Teachers are often guilty of not supporting newly appointed supervisors in their quest for competence and, at times, even throw up roadblocks to hinder the success of new administrators. Supervisors and mentors can be guilty of not believing in the capacity of teachers to grow and change. Having a common goal of student and adult learning, taking time to build professional relationships, being purposeful about demonstrating benevolence and competence, and about looking for evidence of benevolence and competence in others are essential components of making the supervision and evaluation process make a difference.

The Power of Conversations

Sit and get ain't it! Interview any educator and you will hear that there is never enough time to talk about the art and craft of teaching, learning, and leading. Yet we continue to attend, and even plan such meetings, professional development events, and supervision and evaluation conferences where we do just that. Somehow, there are those among us who manage to make time not only informal conversations, but find time for data driven discussions and to make plans about what to do next. Monthly face to face interactions focused on teaching and learning combined with frequent short shared teaching and learning episodes and the use of data to inform those discussions and classroom visits has great potential. Naturally, all this talk has to result in action!

The Future of
Supervision and Evaluation
The Case for Differentiated Supervision and Evaluation

"If the purpose of evaluating teachers is to improve teaching and learning, and we believe it is, then schools are not getting the dividends in teacher professional growth for the amount of time now spent on evaluation. We found that limited resources and competing priorities are impetus enough for rethinking teacher evaluation procedures. When coupled with contemporary research about supervision and evaluation, it became evident that having teachers work with each other, and in partnership with supervisors is more effective than traditional evaluation procedures for improving classroom practice."

Teaching Matters: Strengthening Teacher Evaluation in Massachusetts

The above quote from a position paper by MassPartners for Public Schools, February, 2002 says it all! When the seven Massachusetts associations representing teachers, principals, superintendents, school committees, and parents agree that we need to rethink how we supervise and evaluate professional educators, we are on to something big!

Differentiated Supervision
- Is based on adult learning theory and the research on change
- Recognizes the stages of professional development through which all teachers move
- Provides an opportunity for teachers and evaluators to be more collegial in their interactions, so that they and the students learn and grow
- Increases the likelihood that teachers will engage in action research and apply the results of the research in their classroom
- Validates and supports the importance of teacher collaboration
- Continues to provide avenues for remediation
- In most instances, meets contractual obligations at the district level, as well as, fulfilling state requirements

The following pages present excerpts from Greece Central School District, Greece New York, and from the Missouri Department of Education documents that represent the alternative approaches to supervision and evaluation of tenured teachers they are using.

Examples of
Differentiated Supervision and Evaluation

Greece Central School District, Greece, New York, offers an Alternative Professional Performance Review. To be eligible for an alternative option in a given year, the supervisor(s) and tenured teacher mutually agree to participate. The purpose of an Alternative Professional Performance Review is to encourage staff to identify a means to evaluate contributions made on an annual basis that are aligned with the teacher Professional Performance Review Criteria.

Alternative Professional Review Options

Reflective Teaching Partners

Two teachers work collaboratively to assess teaching methods and their affect on the students (i.e., supervising a students teacher, mentoring a teacher). For example, one teacher may agree to collect information while visiting his/her partner's classroom. After the visit, the teachers meet to discuss their findings. Then they reverse roles.

Peer Coaching

This is a collaborative technique that provides opportunities for teachers working together to practice developing competency on a specific teaching technique or strategy. Peer coaching often has a narrow focus, and helps to facilitate the early use of a skill or strategy that has been presented to teachers as part of their professional development training.

Learning Club

Two or more teachers study an educational topic or issue to explore the instructional implications, and then apply the skill within the context of their instructional setting.

Action Research

One or more teachers collect impact data demonstrating the effects of practice on learning or behavior. A process of identifying an issue, modifying practice, and reevaluation occurs.

Examples of
Differentiated Supervision and Evaluation
Alternative Professional Review Options
Greece Central School District
Portfolio

The portfolio provides teachers with a framework for innovative ways to document performance. A teaching portfolio contains any items that an education selects to put in it. Through the process of collecting, selecting, and reflecting,, the portfolio becomes a tool for an individual Professional Development Plan.

Professional portfolios may include:

- An outcome statement that forms the basis for the portfolio. All materials selected to be included should support and document that outcome
- Examples of student work that support the outcome
- Information from others such as: awards, newspaper articles, letters from parents or students, or any other documents that demonstrate student progress
- Narrative by the teacher as to how and why the items in the portfolio support the outcome

Self Reflection

Self-reflection offers a teacher a continuous, ongoing process of professional growth that fosters the improvement of instruction, the teaching/learning processes, and the overall school climate. Reflections upon strengths, as well as areas of potential growth will be discussed. Self-reflection may include participants in a workshop, course, conference, or seminar that includes a self-evalaution or professional growth planning component.

The steps for this self-reflection model may include:

- Identified outcome
- Evaluation of how the teacher's performance supports the outcome
- A comment section as to how and why the examples support the teacher's philosophy

Other

This open category allows a teacher to be innovative in developing a personal plan for professional/instructional growth.

Differentiated Supervision and Evaluation
Missouri Professional Development Options

Important to Note: A requirement of all options offered to tenured teachers is that the plan and the products must relate to specific performance criteria and to school improvement goals.

Mentor Teacher

A teacher participates in mentor training offered by the district, documents and reflects on his/her interactions with a first or second year teacher in a way that relates the learning to his/her own practice. The mentor teacher assists the novice teacher with the development of the portfolio required of all first and second year teachers.

Action Research Team

Two to five colleagues work together toward a common goal. The area of research might be an issue or strategy or theme such as increasing student attendance, literacy, or extended instructional periods. Each team member maintains data to document the research. Documentation options are broad; three different perspectives on the area of research are required.

Individual Professional Activity

A teacher works on an area as approved by the supervisor. This work might focus on curriculum development, program development, or use of technology.

Professional Review Process

The teacher is videotaped during three or more teaching sessions, focusing on one or more criteria and self-assesses the lesson in writing. The teacher can also have a peer, supervisor, or induction coach observe a lesson. The observation and the conference with the outside observer would be documented in writing. The teacher's portfolio would document the observations, the data gathered and analyzed, as well as summary reflections on professional growth during the process.

Examples of
Differentiated Supervision and Evaluation

Collaborative Professional Plan

A teacher interacts with colleagues focusing on particular teaching behavior. This could be accomplished through peer coaching, a study group, or other forms of collaborative teams.

School-Wide or District-Wide Action Research

Teachers with significant experience work collaboratively on a project outlined in a school/building school improvement plan. Teams may represent a specific grade level, subject, or cross discipline/cross district teams. Examples of such projects might be developing of tasks to evaluate programs or curriculum implementation.

Leading
the
Learning
Areas of Professional
Performance

Areas of Performance
Frameworks
Ideas to Try
Best Practices to Note
Suggestions to Make
Self-Assessments and Reflections
Questions to Ask
Resources

This section provides support for teachers, mentors, coaches, and supervisors in their efforts to make meaning of district teacher performance criteria by providing **look fors** and **think abouts**. The essential questions addressed are:

- What decisions, behaviors, and questions promote teacher growth and student learning?
- What does it look and sound like when teaching and learning is centered on the high achievement of all students?
- How do we organize our thinking and analysis of teaching and learning?

Examples of
Areas/Standards of Performance

Both Judith Warren Little in a paper published in the Fall 1982 **American Educational Research Journal** and Jon Saphier in **How to Make Supervision and Evaluation Really Work** made important contributions to the body of work around collegial practice and supervision and evaluation when they advocated for a common language and concept system to be shared by teachers and supervisors. The standards-based movement that led to **clearly articulated expectations for students** provided the foundation for most states and school districts to more **clearly articulate expectations for teachers and administrators**. While there are differences in the organizational systems of the performance criteria, there are far more similarities than differences.

Charlotte Danielson's work **Enhancing Professional Practice** has greatly influenced how criteria for teacher performance is organized, as has the work of the **National Board of Professional Teaching Standards** and **The Council of Chief State School Officers** that began its work with model standards for beginning teacher licensing and is now extending that work in to content areas.

No matter how performance standards are organized, there are always overlaps between and among the standards. In the introduction of the California Standards for the Teaching Profession, the writers explain these overlaps by stating:

> **"These overlaps are intended to underscore the holistic view that emphasizes the interrelationships and complexities of teaching."**

A sampling of organizational structures of performance standards or domains is presented below.

Texas Professional Development and Appraisal System (PDAS)
- Active, Successful Student Participation in the Learning Process
- Learner-Centered Instruction
- Evaluation and Feedback on Student Progress
- Management of Student Discipline, Instructional Strategies, Time/Materials
- Professional Communication
- Professional Development
- Compliance with Policies, Operating Procedures, and Requirements
- Improvement of All Students' Academic Performance

Examples of
Areas/Standards of Performance

Massachusetts Professional Standards for Teachers
- Plans Curriculum and Instruction
- Delivers Effective Instruction
- Manages Classroom Climate and Operations
- Promotes Equity and an Appreciation of Diversity
- Meets Professional Responsibilities

Virginia Guidelines for Uniform Performance Standards and Evaluation Criteria
- Planning and Assessment
- Instruction
- Safety and Learning Environment
- Communication and Community Relations
- Professionalism

California Standards for the Teaching Profession
- Engaging and Supporting All Students in Learning
- Creating and Maintaining Effective Environments for Student Learning
- Understanding and Organizing Subject Matter for Student Learning
- Planning Instruction and Designing Learning Experiences for All Students
- Assessing Student Learning
- Developing as a Professional Educator

New York State Criteria for Professional Performance
- Content Knowledge
- Preparation
- Instructional Delivery
- Classroom Management
- Student Development
- Student Assessment
- Collaboration
- Reflective and Responsive Practice

Performance-Based Standards for Colorado Teachers
- Knowledge of Literacy
- Knowledge of Mathematics
- Knowledge of Standards and Assessment
- Knowledge of Classroom and Instructional Management
- Knowledge of Individualization of Instruction
- Knowledge of Technology
- Democracy, Education Governance, and Careers in Teaching

ASK Framework for The Study of Teaching and Learning

The **ASK Framework** presented here and on the following pages is based on an analysis of areas of performance or domains developed by organizations, districts, and school systems. The headings or categories used in a given district may vary slightly from the six present here; however, the components are almost universal.

While this chapter is organized around these six areas of performance, readers should use the documents developed by their own districts to analyze teaching and learning episodes and teacher decision making. Time and energy spent aligning the information presented here with district documents is an excellent way to better understand the content and intent of the district documents.

In the absence of a clearly articulated district criteria for teacher performance, this framework can serve as a starting point for development of a district framework. It is not written in outcomes language, but rather identifies components to be considered so would need to be modified to read as such.

ASK Framework for The Study of Teaching and Learning

Planning Instruction

Standards-Based Teaching, Learning, and Assessment

Lesson, Unit and Course Design

Content Specific Pedagogy

Learning Styles, Multiple Intelligences and Brain Research

Diversity of Students

Active Learning

Connections to the World Beyond the Classroom

Integration of the Curriculum

Implementing Instruction

Framing the Learning

Dealing with Naive Understandings and Misconceptions

Communicating Purposes, Expectations, and Directions

Using a Repertoire of Strategies, Materials, and Resources

Designing Rigorous Questions and Assignments Aligned with Desired Outcomes

Promoting Connections and Meaning Making

Incorporating Literacy Instruction

Differentiating Instruction

Accommodating and Adapting for Special Needs Students

Assessing Learning and the Instructional Program

The Assessment Continuum

Checking for Understanding

Designing, Selecting, and Assessing Paper and Pencil Assessments

Designing, Selecting, Implementing, and Assessing Performance Tasks

Designing and Using Rubrics and Performance Assessment Task Lists

Using Assessment Results to Inform Teaching Decisions

ASK Framework for The Study of Teaching and Learning

Orchestrating a Positive Learning Environment

Building a Community of Learners

Having and Communicating High Expectations to All Students

Using Attribution Theory to Reframe Belief Systems

Building Capacity Through Learning How to Learn Strategies

Using Errors and/or Lack of Background Knowledge and Skills as Learning Opportunities

Building in Reflection and Metacognition

Developing Thinking Skills for the 21st Century

Building Appropriate and Positive Personal Relationships with Students

Organizing and Leading a Productive Learning-Centered Environment

Creating and Using Organizational Systems for Professional and Instructional Materials

Developing and Implementing Organizational Systems for Learners and the Classroom

Planning Proactively to Work with Reluctant and Resistant Learners

Professionalism and Collegial Collaboration

The Ways We Collaborate: Consultant, Collaborator, and Coach

Formats for Collaboration and Job-Embedded Learning

Peer Observation

Mentoring

Co-Teaching

Professional Responsibilities

Parents as Partners

ASK Framework for The Study of Teaching and Learning

Each of the areas of performance represented in **The ASK Framework** are explored in depth on the following pages.

Information on each area includes:

- Ideas for teachers to try to improve their own practice
- Best practices for supervisors, mentors, and coaches to note
- Suggestions supervisors, mentors, and coaches might make
- Questions and queries to provide focus and promote reflective practice by teachers as they engage in either the supervision and evaluation process or in collaborative initiatives, including peer observation and action research.
- Where to find support materials in *Instruction for All Students* and *Why Didn't I Learn This in College?*

Additional Support for Reflective Practice

- More questions to use in planning and reflective conferences are found on pages 193 and 195-196 plus **Tool-15: Providing Context for Formal Observations**.
- See **Tool-27: Student Impact Plan** for reflective questions to use in designing professional growth plans and in analyzing the results of those plans.
- The best practices to note can also be used to design professional growth or student impact plans.
- See formats for professional growth plans at **Tool-25: ASK Goal Setting, Tool-26: Improvement of Student Achievement Plan, Tool-27: Student Impact Plan, Tool-31: Improvement Plan**.
- See **Tool-30: Teacher Candidate Interview Questions**.

Planning Instruction
Ideas to Try... Best Practices to Note... Suggestions...

> *I want to try to... I want/need to be more purposeful about... I/You might consider... I noticed that... I/You need to... It is likely to promote student achievement if I/You ...*

- Use the **district and state standards** to plan for the year, the unit, and the lesson
- **Use the standards-based planning process to plan and pace for the year**
- **Use the standards-based planning process for units and lessons** by aligning assessments and learning experiences with the standards
- Identify the **essential understandings, key concepts, and big ideas** of the content areas being taught
- **Design summative assessments prior to planning units or lessons**
- Design learning experiences that give students **practices and rehearsals** at the same level of understanding as the level at which the standards/outcomes are written
- Be clear about how any given **lesson/learning experience is directly related** to the standards/outcomes
- State standards in lesson plans
- **Analyze instructional materials** for match to district outcomes
- **Identify supplemental materials** and design learning experiences to **fill any gaps** in standard materials
- Use the **task analysis process** to identify the knowledge, skills, and level of understanding required by the task
- Include knowledge of student **readiness levels, interests, and learning styles** in designing learning experiences
- Build **pauses for processing** into the lesson design and use 10:2 Theory and Wait Time as guidelines
- Plan and write out the **key questions** to ask during a lesson
- Analyze **text structure** and teach students to use **graphic organizers** to represent the thinking processes used by the author and to capture the key information in the text

Planning
More Ideas to Try... Best Practices to Note...

> *I want to try to... I want/need to be more purposeful about... I/You might consider... I noticed that... I/You need to... It is likely to promote student achievement if I/You ...*

- **Align assignments to include homework with standards and assessments** and be purposeful about **examining homework results for evidence of learning**

- Use **Models of Teaching** such as Bruner's Concept Attainment, Hilda Taba's Inductive Model, Aronson's Jigsaw Classroom, and the Inquiry/Problem Solving Model

- Use the skills and competencies laid out in the **SCANS Report** (Secretary's Commission on Achieving the Necessary Skills) in lesson and unit design

- Eliminate lessons and learning exercises that do not move students toward meeting the standards

- **Collaborate /consult with support staff** about special needs students

- **For special educators:**

  ▶ Use knowledge of **medical conditions and medications** and their possible effects on student learning and behavior to plan instruction

  ▶ Use knowledge of **educational disabilities and giftedness** and their effects on student learning needs to individualize instruction

See Chapter II in *Instruction for All Students* and Chapter VII in *Why Didn't I Learn This in College?* for information on planning.

Planning Instruction
Reflections and Questions...

How might I/you...? How do I/ you feel it went when I/you...? Why do I/you think that is so? What did I/you learn from the situation in which I/you...? What does the data/research tell me/you about ...?

- Describe your **efforts to master the state standards and the district outcomes** in your field/at your grade level.

- How have you used your **knowledge of state standards and district outcomes to the planning, implementation, and evaluation of instructional programs?**

- Describe the factors you consider and the methods you use to formulate **lesson objectives.**

- Describe the factors you consider in lesson and unit design.

- How do you combine **personal practical experience and research** to make instructional decisions?

- What are your systems for ensuring that **instruction focuses on what standards students need to achieve** instead of on what is fun to teach or is readily available in a textbook?

- Explain how **content specific pedagogy** impacts your planning?

- What is the process you use to identify essential understandings and then use those understandings to plan instruction and assess learning?

- Who/what has the **greatest influence on the planning decisions** you make around instruction, assessment, and the environment? Why do you think these are the most influential?

- What are the **key concepts, big ideas, or essential understandings** of the content you are teaching?

- How do you ensure that you present **different points of view and a variety of cultural perspectives?**

- How do you use **preassessment data and/or students' prior knowledge in the planning process?**

Planning Instruction

Professionalism & Collegial Collaboration

Implementing Instruction

Organizing a Productive Environment

Assessing Learning & the Instructional Program

Orchestrating a Positive Environment

Planning Instruction
More Reflections and Questions...

> *How might I/you...? How do I/ you feel it went when I/you...? Why do I/you think that is so? What did I/you learn from the situation in which I/you...? What does the data/research tell me/you about ...?*

- How do you go about **evaluating teaching resources and materials** for comprehensiveness, accuracy, potential for student engagement, and their match to the learning standards?

- What are the **variables** you consider when planning for **differentiation of instruction**?

- How do you use your knowledge of **Multiple Intelligences theory and learning styles to design learning experiences** that will engage all learners?

- What is the process you use to create **interdisciplinary learning experiences** that help students make connections between the various content areas they are studying?

- When planning for the year, what is your process for ensuring that the **level of student work increases between the fall and the spring?**

- How do you think about what you **plan in relationship to both the entire school year and to the K-12 experiences of learners?**

ASK Framework for
The Study of Teaching and Learning

The **ASK Framework** is presented here with notations of support materials found in *Leading the Learning* (Rutherford, 2005), *Why Didn't I Learn This in College?* (Rutherford, 2009), and *Instruction for All Students* (Rutherford, 2008).

Why Didn't I Learn This in College? is written for novice teachers and their supervisors, mentors, and coaches. The content focuses on planning, instruction, building a learning community, and creating and implementing organizational systems for effective learning in a learning-centered classroom. *Instruction for All Students* builds on that work and extends the study of teaching and learning to include differentiation of instruction, 21st century thinking skills, and collegial collaboration.

Planning Instruction

Standards-Based Teaching, Learning, and Assessment
Instruction for All Students pages 28-30 and 34-42
Why Didn't I Learn This in College? pages 172-183

Lesson, Unit, and Course Design
Instruction for All Students Chapter II, pages 31 to 54
Why Didn't I Learn This in College? Chapter VII, pages 169-192

Learning Styles, Multiple Intelligences, and Brain Research
Instruction for All Students pages 7, 50, and 127-132

Diversity of Students
Why Didn't I Learn This in College? pages 39-42 and 131-132

Active Learning
Instruction for All Students Chapter IV, pages 83-120
Why Didn't I Learn This in College? Chapter IV, pages 63-107

Connections to the World Beyond the Classroom
Instruction for All Students pages 135-139, 168, 173, 183-194, 221-223, and 248

Integration of the Curriculum
Instruction for All Students pages 48-49 and 125

Additional Resources on
Planning Instruction

Planning Instruction

Professionalism & Collegial Collaboration

Implementing Instruction

Organizing a Productive Environment

Assessing Learning & the Instructional Program

Orchestrating a Positive Environment

On the Web

- www.askeric.org
- www.sdcoe.k12.ca.us
- webquest.sdsu.edu
- www.eduhelper.com
- www.nytimes.com/learning
- www.teachers.net

In Print

- *Models of Teaching* by Bruce Joyce & Marsha Well
- *Operators Guide to a Standards-Based Classroom* from Centennial Boces, Longmont, Colorado
- *Instruction: A Models Approach* by Mary Alice Gunter, Thomas Estes, & Jan Schwab
- *Understanding By Design* by Grant Wiggins & Jay McTighe
- *The Differentiated Classroom: Responding to the Needs of All Learners* by Carol Ann Tomlinson

Implementing Instruction
Ideas to Try... Best Practices to Note... Suggestions...

> *I want to try to... I want/need to be more purposeful about... I/You might consider... I noticed that... I/You need to... It is likely to promote student achievement if I/You ...*

- **Communicate the standards** and learning objectives **in age appropriate language**
- **Communicate why** what students are learning is **important to know**
- **Communicate how the learning exercises** the students are doing **are related to the learning outcomes**; that is, explain the purpose and relevance of all assignments and learning experiences
- **Communicate how the current lesson is related to and builds on previous lessons**
- **Help students build skills at recognizing how the current lesson is related to and builds on previous lessons**
- **Communicate** to students how their **learning will be assessed**
- **Provide scoring guides** such as rubrics, performance task lists and checklists to students **before they begin working**
- **Provide daily, unit, and semester agendas**
- **Have students access their prior knowledge**
- **Identify student misconceptions and naive understandings**; help students reframe their thinking as appropriate
- Provide or have students provide **connections between what is being learned in the moment with other areas of their study and to life beyond the classroom**
- Present **accurate and current information**
- **Provide multiple illustrations, examples, and comparisons of complex or highly abstract ideas or concepts**
- **Emphasize the key terms/ideas** to be learned
- **Use positive and negative examples** to help identify critical or important attributes

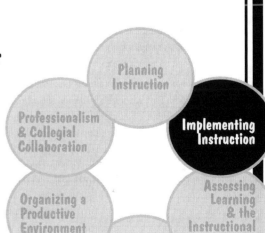

Implementing Instruction
More Ideas to Try... Best Practices to Note... Suggestions...

> *I want to try to... I want/need to be more purposeful about... I/You might consider... I noticed that... I/You need to... It is likely to promote student achievement if I/You ...*

- Whenever possible move from **concrete** (props) **to semi-abstract** (pictures) **to abstract** (words and numbers) in presenting new concepts

- **Model thinking aloud**

- **Use analogies, metaphors, and similes**

- **Use physical models and manipulatives**

- **Use Wait Time I and Wait II**

- **Use segues at transitions** so students can make cognitive connections between points under study and between various learning exercises

- Have students **make predictions** about what will happen next or about the next steps they need to take

- **Have students process and summarize learning** at meaningful points

- **Have students assess old predictions, make new predictions, make connections, pose questions, and/or identify significant information at processing points**

- **Use 10:2 Theory** as a time template for student processing

- **Supplement lectures** with colorful transparencies, Power Point-type presentations, models, charts, graphs, and other **visual aids**

- **Enhance lectures with discussion partners, graphic organizers, learning logs, etc.**

- **Check for understanding** throughout lessons by asking questions students can answer only if they truly understand concepts and/or the reasons for the processes

- **Assign homework** for which students have the prerequisite skills to complete the **work independently with an 80% success rate**

Planning Instruction

Professionalism & Collegial Collaboration

Implementing Instruction

Organizing a Productive Environment

Orchestrating a Positive Environment

Assessing Learning & the Instructional Program

Implementing Instruction
More Ideas to Try... Best Practices to Note... Suggestions...

> *I want to try to... I want/need to be more purposeful about... I/You might consider... I noticed that... I/You need to... It is likely to promote student achievement if I/You ...*

- **Assign homework from all four categories**: practice, preparation, extension, and creative to promote both homework completion, learning, and engagement
- **Go beyond recording completion of homework; use successful/unsuccessful completion as formative assessment data to inform teaching decisions**
- Gather and make accessible **multiple sources of information** such as books, magazines, journals, posters, pictures, charts, graphs, maps, and technology
- **Differentiate instruction** by providing a variety of sources, learning processes, and ways to demonstrate learning
- **Use flexible groupings** based on readiness levels, interests, student choice, and learning styles
- **Change strategies as necessary** to meet students' learning needs
- **Integrate content with cross-curricular themes and skills**

Focus on
Rigorous Instruction and Thinking Skills
Ideas to Try... Best Practices to Note... Suggestions...

I want to try to... I want/need to be more purposeful about... I/You might consider... I noticed that... I/You need to... It is likely to promote student achievement if I/You ...

- **Use Bloom's Taxonomy** and the Question and Task Wheel to purposefully design questions and tasks at a variety of cognitive levels
- **Ask all students questions that require higher levels of thinking and probe student answers** for clarification and extension
- **Pose open-ended thought-provoking questions**
- **Name, model, and provide practice of thinking processes** so that students can build and independently access their own thinking skills repertoire
- Have students identify where else a particular thinking skill might be useful and **design tasks so that they use these thinking skills in multiple situations**
- **Teach students** to use journals, learning logs, or interactive notebooks to **analyze and reflect on their own learning and the effectiveness of their effort**
- **Use Williams' Taxonomy of Effective and Creative Thinking** to design questions and learning tasks
- **Have students analyze print text, media, and technological sources for reliability and relevance**
- Include opportunities for both **inductive and deductive thinking**
- **Teach skills of inquiry**
- **Teach skills of dialogue and debate**
- Point out, or have students identify, **how ideas are alike and different and how they relate to one another**
- Have students **seek evidence/data to support opinions and generalizations**
- Have students demonstrate **relevant and important connections they are making**

For information on 21ˢᵗ Century Thinking Skills see Chapter IX, pages 217-248, in *Instruction for All Students*.

Planning Instruction

Professionalism & Collegial Collaboration

Implementing Instruction

Organizing a Productive Environment

Assessing Learning & the Instructional Program

Orchestrating a Positive Environment

Focus on
Constructivist Instruction
Ideas to Try... Best Practices to Note... Suggestions...

I want to try to... I want/need to be more purposeful about... I/You might consider... I noticed that... I/You need to... It is likely to promote student achievement if I/You ...

- Encourage **students to talk about ideas with other students**
- Encourage students to **think about how the information they are learning relates to other subjects and their lives beyond the school day**
- Have students **think critically and creatively** by asking questions that have more than one answer
- **Encourage students to think and discuss answers with a partner or a small group before answering in the larger group**
- Help students **explore and build on their ideas**
- Ensure that class time spent on practice exercises and learning the facts leads to **meaningful use of the facts and skills** in the near future
- **Ask students what they already know about a unit before introducing it**
- **Use essential questions and key concepts to** help students organize new information in ways that make sense to them
- Have students **take sides on issues and explain points of view**
- Have students **resolve their differences by discussing their thinking**
- **Encourage students to try solving difficult problems, even before they learn all the material**
- **Allow students to explore topics that excite or interest them**
- Design assessments around **real world applications**
- **Have students help determine how they demonstrate learning and how they are assessed**

Planning Instruction

Professionalism & Collegial Collaboration

Implementing Instruction

Organizing a Productive Environment

Assessing Learning & the Instructional Program

Orchestrating a Positive Environment

Focus on
Small Group Work/Cooperative Learning
Ideas to Try... Best Practices to Note... Suggestions...

I want to try to... I want/need to be more purposeful about... I/You might consider... I noticed that... I/You need to... It is likely to promote student achievement if I/You ...

- Ensure that the work is **rigorous, worthy of the time, and aligned with desired outcomes**
- **Give directions that apply to all in the large group; when directions apply only to certain groups, give directions via task cards at learning centers or as handouts**
- **Model and practice student movement** so that students move quickly and smoothly into groups
- Provide direction and practice so that **students stay with their group** rather than wandering around
- **Encourage students to help each other answer questions and solve problems** rather than relying on the teacher to answer all questions and solve all problems
- Monitor whether or not all students in the groups are **working on the task equally and adjust accordingly**
- **Consider assigning roles** to students **and rotating those roles** so that all students are given the opportunity to develop the skills necessary for success in that role
- **Intervene in both academic and process situations** as appropriate while allowing students to resolve issues when possible
- **Offer responses that promote student solving of problems** rather than teacher solving of problems
- **Build in individual accountability** rather than relying on group grades
- **Use flexible grouping;** consider readiness, gender, learning style, interests, and student choice as variables
- **Answer questions with a question**
- Teach, model, and review the **interaction/social skills** needed for successful work and learning
- Have students review the **effectiveness and efficiency of the group process** and make plans for improvement

See pages 53-54 in *Instruction for All Students* for information on cooperative learning and pages 249-256 in *Why Didn't I Learn This in College?* for information on small group work.

Planning Instruction

Professionalism & Collegial Collaboration

Implementing Instruction

Organizing a Productive Environment

Assessing Learning & the Instructional Program

Orchestrating a Positive Environment

Focus on
Literacy Instruction Across the Curriculum
Ideas to Try... Best Practices to Note... Suggestions...

I want to try to... I want/need to be more purposeful about... I/You might consider... I noticed that... I/You need to... It is likely to promote student achievement if I/You ...

- Create a **text rich environment** by collecting, displaying, and using a wide variety of books, magazines, posters, etc., in the classroom

- Provide opportunities for **students to locate, organize, and use information from various sources** to answer questions, solve problems, and communicate ideas

- **Use diverse fiction and non-fiction sources** to include many authors and perspectives, as well as children's and young adult literature

- **Teach reading as a process of constructing meaning** through the interaction of the reader's prior knowledge and experiences, the information presented in the text, and the context/purpose of the reading

- **Teach affixes, prefixes, and common roots** used frequently in the content area

- Identify **independent, instructional, and frustration reading levels** of groups and individuals and plan assignments accordingly

- Provide opportunities for students to:
  - **Speak** for a variety of purposes and audiences
  - **Listen** in a variety of situations to information from a variety of sources
  - **Write** in clear, concise, organized language that varies in content and form for different audiences and purposes
  - **Read** various materials and texts with comprehension and critical analysis
  - **View, understand, and use** nontextual visual information (NJ Core Curriculum)

See Chapter V: Integrating Literacy Instruction in *Why Didn't I Learn This in College?* and pages 14-19, 78-80, 88-89 in *Instruction for All Students.*

Focus on
Literacy Instruction Across the Curriculum
More Ideas to Try... Best Practices to Note... Suggestions...

> *I want to try to... I want/need to be more purposeful about... I/You might consider... I noticed that... I/You need to... It is likely to promote student achievement if I/You ...*

- Provide a **balanced literacy program** that includes reading to students, reading with students, independent reading by students, writing for and with students, and writing by students
- **Analyze and evaluate instructional materials** by considering readability, content, length, format, cultural orientation, and illustrations/visuals
- Use a reading approach aligned with the **No Child Left Behind Act of 2001** to include **phonemic awareness, phonics, vocabulary development, reading fluency, including oral reading skills and reading comprehension strategies**

Planning Instruction

Professionalism & Collegial Collaboration

Implementing Instruction

Organizing a Productive Environment

Orchestrating a Positive Environment

Assessing Learning & the Instructional Program

Focus on
Instruction in Inclusive Classrooms
Ideas to Try... Best Practices to Note... Suggestions...

> *I want to try to... I want/need to be more purposeful about... I/You might consider... I noticed that... I/You need to... It is likely to promote student achievement if I/You ...*

- **Task analyze** all assignments and assessments
- Provide **special education students an expanded curriculum** including communication skills, oral language development, social/behavior skills, motor skills, and self-advocacy skills
- Include **explicit instruction that is structured, sequential, and cumulative** in the development of skills
- **Break complex tasks into simpler parts** and then put the complex task back together
- **Use backward chaining**
- **Use think alouds** and then guide students in using the skills or processes modeled in the think aloud
- In co-teaching situations
  - ►Ensure that all professional interactions between the general education and special education teachers cause the two to be seen by all as equal partners rather than having the special educator appear to function as a paraprofessional
  - ►Consider the messages about teacher roles and relationships sent in parent communication
  - ►Be clear about who is taking responsibility for what parts of the planning
  - ►Decide in advance how the lesson will be structured and who will do what
  - ►Share responsibility for developing procedures, expectations, and grading/critiquing students' work
  - ►Decide who will do which tasks in an equitable way

See *Instruction for All Students* pages 195-216 and *Why Didn't I Learn This in College?* pages 39-42, 173-174.

Planning Instruction

Professionalism & Collegial Collaboration

Implementing Instruction

Organizing a Productive Environment

Orchestrating a Positive Environment

Assessing Learning & the Instructional Program

Focus on
Differentiated Instruction
Ideas to Try... Best Practices to Note... Suggestions...

I want to try to... I want/need to be more purposeful about... I/You might consider... I noticed that... I/You need to... It is likely to promote student achievement if I/You ...

- Keep learning and assessment for all students focused on **essential to know concepts and skills** as identified in state and district standards

- **Differentiate instructional support systems but not expectations for student learning**

- Ensure that learning experiences and types and degree of teacher support are selected based on a **task analysis** that includes an analysis of the **skills and knowledge embedded in the task** plus the **level of understanding** required by the task

- Use an analysis of **student readiness/background knowledge levels, interests,** and **information processing styles** to identify appropriate learning experiences and teacher support systems

- **Provide sources of information** at various reading levels, in different languages, and in varying formats to match the needs of learners

- **Engage all students** in **meaningful tasks** that provide balance between skill building and meaning making

- Provide **a balance of student and teacher choice** of working conditions, sources of information, methods of processing learning, and demonstrating that learning

- Use a variety of instruction approaches to include **individual, small group, and whole class instruction**

- **Use flexible grouping;** create groups based on a variety of factors, including readiness levels and interests

- **Give students precise, public, and prior guidelines for assignments, performance tasks, assessments, and behavior**

- **Provide models or exemplars of products and teach and model processes**

For information on differentiation of instruction see Chapter VIII, pages 195-216, in *Instruction for All Students.*

Focus on
Sheltered Instruction for ELLs
Ideas to Try... Best Practices to Note... Suggestions...

I want to try to... I want/need to be more purposeful about... I/You might consider... I noticed that... I/You need to... It is likely to promote student achievement if I/You ...

- Be thoughtful and purposeful in the use of **academic/school related language** such as direction giving and content specific vocabulary

- Be mindful of **slang or colloquialisms** in teacher and classmates' speech

- Use **concrete objects, models, and demonstrations** to support instruction

- Provide **visual cues** to support understanding

- Build in **movement, rhythm, and repetition** to support retention

- **Analyze and evaluate instructional materials** considering readability, content, length, format, cultural orientation, and illustrations/visuals

- Use the **writing strategies included in balanced literacy programs,** such as shared writing, interactive writing, guided writing, and short independent writing sessions in early years of developing English language skills

- Use what is known about students' families, cultures, and communities as a basis for **connecting instruction to students' personal experiences**

- **Provide multiple perspectives,** including attention to students' personal, family, and community experiences and cultural norms

- **Ask questions as simply and concisely as possible**

- **Ask questions that require more than one word answers**

- Encourage all students to **answer in complete sentences** so that second language learners hear the answer in context and learn the rhythm of the English

- **Use wait time** before calling on any student and after any student answers so that processing and any necessary translation can occur

- **Ask second language learners to retell, paraphrase, and summarize** discussion and reading points to promote comprehension and fluency

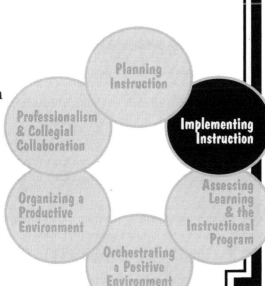

Focus on
Sheltered Instruction for ELLs
Ideas to Try... Best Practices to Note... Suggestions...

I want to try to... I want/need to be more purposeful about... I/You might consider... I noticed that... I/You need to... It is likely to promote student achievement if I/You ...

- **Assign roles in small group work** to ensure that second language learners are active participants
- **Break complex tasks into simpler parts** by providing second language learners oral directions one step at time until they can follow two and three part directions independently

Planning
Instruction

Professionalism
& Collegial
Collaboration

Implementing
Instruction

Organizing a
Productive
Environment

Assessing
Learning
& the
Instructional
Program

Orchestrating
a Positive
Environment

See Chapter V, pages 110, 112, and 131-132 in *Why Didn't I Learn This in College?*

Implementing Instruction
Reflections and Questions

How might I/you...? How do I/ you feel it went when I/you...? Why do I/you think that is so? What did I/you learn from the situation in which I/you...? What does the data/research tell me/you about ...?

- How do you find out **what students already know** about what they are about to read/study?

- How do you ensure that students access what they know and **have experiences with both inside and outside the classroom** as it relates to what they are about to read/study?

- How do you help them not only **build on prior experiences** but **reframe their thinking** when appropriate?

- Describe how you provide opportunities for students to make **real-world connections** from their learning

- Describe two or three situations when you **adjusted instruction based on student questions, misconceptions, naive understandings, or interests**

- Given your current student population, describe how you **select the presentation modes** to use in introducing new material

- How do presentation modes and learning experiences move from **concrete to abstract?**

- Describe how you **create, access, select, and adapt materials** and equipment to facilitate learning

- What are the ways in which you use **technology as a learning tool?**

- How do you **select the examples, stories, and props** for use in introducing, reinforcing, or extending understanding of new information?

- How do you **ensure that the explanations or examples are relevant** and that the **references have meaning** for students?

- What might you do to **extend and expand the thinking** of students ready to and/or interested in going beyond what is planned?

Planning Instruction

Professionalism & Collegial Collaboration

Implementing Instruction

Organizing a Productive Environment

Assessing Learning & the Instructional Program

Orchestrating a Positive Environment

Implementing Instruction
More Reflections and Questions

How might I/you...? How do I/ you feel it went when I/you...? Why do I/you think that is so? What did I/you learn from the situation in which I/you...? What does the data/research tell me/you about ...?

- How do you use **technology as a learning tool?**

- What do you know from your own learning experiences about the fact that **"one size of learning does not fit all?"**

- What do you know about your **struggling, resistant, or reluctant learners** that you need to address up front?

- Describe the various ways you **configure small groups and the variables you consider in those configurations?**

- How is the **rationale for grouping explained to students?**

- How do you **plan the questions** you use to:
  - initiate discussions and keep them on track
  - pique student curiosity
  - help students make connections
  - check for understanding
  - cause students to think critically by evaluating credibility of sources and strength of evidence, to consider alternative viewpoints, and to challenge the obvious

- How do you **reconcile differentiation of instruction with holding all students to the achievement of high standards?**

- What instructional strategies do you have in your **repertoire for helping students who do not grasp/understand the content or process the first time** it is presented and practiced?

- Describe how you vary **your role as instructor, facilitator, coach, or audience** in your interactions with students

See pages 194-195 in the Feedback Section for additional questions to use at reflective conferences.

Planning Instruction

Professionalism & Collegial Collaboration

Implementing Instruction

Organizing a Productive Environment

Assessing Learning & the Instructional Program

Orchestrating a Positive Environment

ASK Framework for
The Study of Teaching and Learning

The **ASK Framework** is presented here with notations of support materials found in *Leading the Learning* (Rutherford, 2005), *Why Didn't I Learn This in College?* (Rutherford, 2009), and *Instruction for All Students* (Rutherford, 2008).

Why Didn't I Learn This in College? is written for novice teachers and their supervisors, mentors, and coaches. The content focuses on planning, instruction, building a learning community, and creating and implementing organizational systems for effective learning in a learning-centered classroom. *Instruction for All Students* builds on that work and extends the study of teaching and learning to include differentiation of instruction, 21st century thinking skills, and collegial collaboration.

Implementing Instruction

Framing the Learning
   Instruction for All Students pages 36, 38, 41, 57-62
   Why Didn't I Learn This in College? pages 48-51

Dealing with Naive Understandings and Misconceptions
   Instruction for All Students pages 59, 64, 107, 110-111, 113
   Why Didn't I Learn This in College? pages 49, 66, 68, 78, 81-82, 89, 98

Communicating Purposes, Expectations, and Directions
   Instruction for All Students pages 58, 251, 258
   Why Didn't I Learn This in College? pages 12-19 and 233

Using a Repertoire of Strategies, Materials, and Resources
   Instruction for All Students...the book!
   Why Didn't I Learn This in College?...the book!

Designing Rigorous Questions and Assignments Aligned with Desired Outcomes
   Instruction for All Students pages 9, 12-13, 219-221, 235, 248
   Why Didn't I Learn This in College? pages 54-56, 60

Promoting Connections and Meaning Making
   Instruction for All Students pages 63-108 and 135-140
   Why Didn't I Learn This in College? pages 63-106

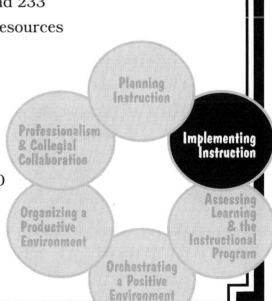

Framework for
The Study of Teaching and Learning

Additional Resources on
Implementing Instruction

- *Classroom Strategies That Work* by Robert Marzano, Debra Pickering, and Diane Pollack

- *The Skillful Teacher* by Jon Saphier and Bob Gower

- *Activators* by Jon Saphier and Mary Ann Haley

- *Summarizers* by Jon Saphier and Mary Ann Haley

- *Strategies that Work* by Stephanie Harvey and Anne Gouvis

- *The Art of Teaching Reading* by Lucy McCormick

- *Mosaic of Thought* by Ellin Oliver Keene and Susan Zimmerman

- *Put Reading First* from the National Institute for Literacy. Download at www.nifl.gov

- *Literature Circles* by Harvey Daniels

Assessing Learning and the Instructional Program
Ideas to Try... Best Practices to Note... Suggestions...

> *I want to try to... I want/need to be more purposeful about... I/You might consider... I noticed that... I/You need to... It is likely to promote student achievement if I/You ...*

- **Go beyond grading student work to critiquing and analyzing student work** to see which components of the standards are at mastery, which are progressing, and which are in need of teaching and reteaching

- **Select assessment tools from a wide range of options** including, but not limited to, paper and pencil assessments

- Do a **preassessment** as part of the planning for a unit of study

- **Design rubrics, performance task lists, and checklists** that articulate in precise language performance and assessment requirements

- **Provide students with clear criteria and exemplars** of processes and products before they begin the work

- **Check for understanding** across all students by using signal cards, slates, think pads, choral responses, and circulation and adjust instruction accordingly

- **Provide formative rehearsals for summative assessments at appropriate levels of thinking**

- **Design and give assignments, to include homework, that provide practice and rehearsals and then analyze the results**

- Include **student self-assessment of products and of the effectiveness of the effort**

- **Teach students** to give each other feedback through **peer editing and review**

- **Use every assignment as data** on what to teach next and to whom and in what ways

- **Engage students in the design of assessment criteria**

- Have **students score anonymous work** to help them understand what the scoring criteria looks like in student work

Planning Instruction

Professionalism & Collegial Collaboration

Implementing Instruction

Organizing a Productive Environment

Assessing Learning & the Instructional Program

Orchestrating a Positive Environment

Assessing Learning and the Instructional Program
More Ideas to Try... Best Practices to Note...

> *I want to try to... I want/need to be more purposeful about... I/You might consider... I noticed that... I/You need to... It is likely to promote student achievement if I/You ...*

- Structure **individual accountability in group work**

- **Monitor impact of teacher behavior** on student success and **modify behavior, plans, and instructional strategies accordingly**

- Describe the **criteria and/or the techniques you use to determine the effectiveness of your instruction**

- **Compare desired outcomes with actual outcomes and adjust plans accordingly**

See Chapter VI in *Why Didn't I Learn This in College?* and Chapter VI in *Instruction for All Students*.

Assessing Learning and the Instructional Program

Reflections and Questions...

> *How might I/you...? How do I/ you feel it went when I/you...? Why do I/you think that is so? What did I/you learn from the situation in which I/you...? What does the data/research tell me/you about ...?*

- How do you use **the results of classroom assessments** such as tests and performance tasks to plan future instruction?

- How do you use **informal assessment information to make instruction decisions?**

- How do you use **standardized test results to make decisions** about the instructional program?

- How do you ensure that the **classroom assessments** you select or design are **valid measures of the district outcomes?**

- Describe the **process used for development of the evaluation criteria**

- How do you **communicate assessment information to students, other staff, and parents?**

- **How would students describe the evaluation process?**

- How do you **provide opportunities for students** to set goals and assess progress?

- **How are initial attempts to use new processes and information used in establishing the final grade?**

- Describe how you **teach students to assess their own performances**

- How do you ensure that the **feedback** you provide is **focused on specific points** on which students can improve or correct?

- How do you **give feedback/present data** to students about performance so that they can to react to that data and develop skills of self-adjustment?

- How do you ensure that **students are learning and growing from the grading, critiquing, and correcting** you do?

- Describe how you **demonstrate to students how to do the task or project and/or provide them examples of products**

Planning Instruction

Professionalism & Collegial Collaboration

Implementing Instruction

Organizing a Productive Environment

Assessing Learning & the Instructional Program

Orchestrating a Positive Environment

Assessing Learning and the Instructional Program
More Reflections and Questions...

> *How might I/you...? How do I/ you feel it went when I/you...? Why do I/you think that is so? What did I/you learn from the situation in which I/you...? What does the data/research tell me/you about ...?*

- How do you **monitor the balance between negative and positive feedback?**

- Describe the **performance of three students** who demonstrated little learning from the preassessment to the summative assessment. What kinds of errors did they make and what did you do before the next learning experiences to help them improve their efforts and their learning?

- Describe how you collect and use information from **classroom interactions, questions, and analysis of student work as formative assessment data**

See Chapter VI in *Why Didn't I Learn This in College?* And Chapter VI in *Instruction for All Students*.

ASK Framework for
The Study of Teaching and Learning

The **ASK Framework** is presented here with notations of support materials found in **Leading the Learning** (Rutherford, 2005), **Why Didn't I Learn This in College?** (Rutherford, 2009), and **Instruction for All Students** (Rutherford, 2008).

Why Didn't I Learn This in College? is written for novice teachers and their supervisors, mentors, and coaches. The content focuses on planning, instruction, building a learning community, and creating and implementing organizational systems for effective learning in a learning-centered classroom. **Instruction for All Students** builds on that work and extends the study of teaching and learning to include differentiation of instruction, 21st century thinking skills, and collegial collaboration.

Assessing Learning & the Instructional Program

The Assessment Continuum
> **Instruction for All Students** Chapter VI, pages 149-180
> **Why Didn't I Learn This in College?** Chapter VI, pages 137-168

Checking for Understanding
> **Instruction for All Students** pages 89, 154-156
> **Why Didn't I Learn This in College?** pages 67 and 142-146

Designing, Selecting, and Assessing Paper and Pencil Assessments
> **Instruction for All Students** 159-161
> **Why Didn't I Learn This in College?** pages 160-163

Designing, Selecting, Implementing, and Assessing Performance Tasks
> **Instruction for All Students** pages 168-174
> **Why Didn't I Learn This in College?** page 164

Designing and Using Rubrics and Performance Assessment Task Lists
> **Instruction for All Students** pages 169-180
> **Why Didn't I Learn This in College?** pages 165-166

Using Assessment Results to Inform Teaching Decisions
> **Instruction for All Students** pages 22-25, 153, 160-161
> **Leading the Learning** pages 45-50 and 154-156

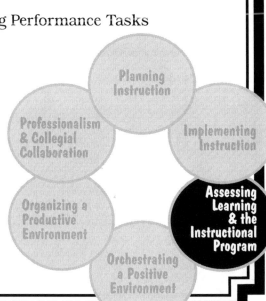

Additional Resources for
Assessing Learning
and the Instructional Program

- *Understanding by Design* by Grant Wiggins and Jay McTighe
- *Performance Based Learning & Assessment* by Educators in Pomeraug Regional School District 15

Planning Instruction

Professionalism & Collegial Collaboration

Implementing Instruction

Organizing a Productive Environment

Assessing Learning & the Instructional Program

Orchestrating a Positive Environment

Positive Learning-Centered Environment
Ideas to Try... Best Practices to Note... Suggestions...

> *I want to try to... I want/need to be more purposeful about... I/You might consider... I noticed that... I/You need to... It is likely to promote student achievement if I/You ...*

- **Learn student names and information about each one** early in the year
- **Greet students at the door with a smile and a handshake**
- **Use student names in examples**
- Make a strong effort to **interact in a positive way with each student each day**
- Develop a system for **monitoring the nature and frequency of your interactions with students**
- Create opportunities for **students to learn about themselves and each other**
- **Be knowledgeable** about the fads, fashions, music, hobbies, sports, and other recreational activities that are **of interest to your students**
- **Display student work** both in the classroom and in public areas; **identify the standard of learning the work represents**
- **Teach students how to set and work toward learning goals**
- Encourage students to **ask for and get help from one another**
- Encourage students to **monitor their own academic progress**
- Set up conditions where **students can assess the effectiveness of their learning habits**
- Teach students to **self-assess the appropriateness and effectiveness of their social skills**
- **Model respect** in words spoken, voice tone, eye contact, and in body language (DoDEA)
- **Use music, books, posters, and pictures from different cultures**
- **Practice equity and explain to students the difference between equity** (get what you need when you need it) **and equality** (all get the same thing at the same time)

Planning Instruction

Professionalism & Collegial Collaboration

Implementing Instruction

Organizing a Productive Environment

Assessing Learning & the Instructional Program

Orchestrating a Positive Environment

Positive Learning-Centered Environment
More Ideas to Try... Best Practices to Note...

> *I want to try to... I want/need to be more purposeful about... I/You might consider... I noticed that... I/You need to... It is likely to promote student achievement if I/You ...*

- Role-play situations with students to **identify appropriate and inappropriate behavior**
- **Provide student choice** of learning process, teach them to make good choices, and analyze why or why not the choices were the best for the learner
- **Explain the reason why you are doing what you are doing or making the decision you are making**
- **Change strategies to meet students' needs rather than expecting students to change to meet teacher needs** (Centennial BOCES)
- Take advantage of opportunities to **use humor**
- Remind yourself that you are a **role model**
- Develop a repertoire of ways to **encourage your students**
- **Reinforce students' attempts to solve problems and exert effort**
- Make it a practice to **recognize effective effort**
- **Resolve behavioral issues privately** with minimum disruption of instruction
- **Avoid sarcasm and ridicule**
- **Promote intrinsic motivation** (I did it!) **rather than extrinsic motivation** (you did it so you get a sticker or piece of candy)
- Show interest in students' lives beyond the classroom by **becoming involved in student activities**
- **Monitor student attributions and use attribution retraining** with those who make external attributions
- **Demonstrate respect for students as individuals** with different personal and family backgrounds and a wide range of skills, talents, and interests.

Orchestrating a Positive Learning-Centered Environment
Reflections and Questions

How might I/you...? How do I/ you feel it went when I/you...? Why do I/you think that is so? What did I/you learn from the situation in which I/you...? What does the data/research tell me/you about ...?

- How do you **engage students in establishing conditions that promote learning for all?**

- How do you provide for **different roles in group work** and how do you ensure that the students carry out those roles?

- What processes do you use to **ensure that students apply and use information rather than simply memorizing facts or processes?**

- How do you **engage students in problem identifying and solving?**

- How do you help students learn to **use collaboration and communication skills in learning situations?**

- How do **students demonstrate enthusiasm, interest, and involvement in their learning?**

- How is **student interest measured?**

- How do you **help students recognize and develop skills to accommodate their own learning styles?**

- How do you **involve students in creating and evaluating their own organizational systems?**

- How would you handle/how have you handled **difficult human relations or a communications problem?**

- How do you **engage students in "ownership" of the classroom** and its smooth operation?

- Describe how you **gather and use information about students' experiences, interests, learning behaviors, needs, and progress from parents, professional colleagues, and the students themselves**

Planning Instruction

Professionalism & Collegial Collaboration

Implementing Instruction

Organizing a Productive Environment

Assessing Learning & the Instructional Program

Orchestrating a Positive Environment

Positive Learning-Centered Environment
More Reflections and Questions

> *How might I/you...? How do I/you feel it went when I/you...? Why do I/you think that is so? What did I/you learn from the situation in which I/you...? What does the data/research tell me/you about ...?*

- How do you **purposefully build on students' interests, needs, and levels of understanding?**

- What opportunities do you provide for **meaningful student choice?**

- How and when do you **build in opportunities for students to reflect on their learning and on the effectiveness of their efforts?**

- How do you use your understanding of **Multiple Intelligences theory and learning styles to help students understand their own and others' learning strengths and needs?**

- How do **students share their work with others?**

- In what ways do you use **your knowledge of group dynamics** to orchestrate the environment in the classroom?

Framework for
The Study of Teaching and Learning

The **ASK Framework** is presented here with notations of support materials found in *Leading the Learning* (Rutherford, 2005), *Why Didn't I Learn This in College?* (Rutherford, 2009), and *Instruction for All Students* (Rutherford, 2008).

Why Didn't I Learn This in College? is written for novice teachers and their supervisors, mentors, and coaches. The content focuses on planning, instruction, building a learning community, and creating and implementing organizational systems for effective learning in a learning-centered classroom. *Instruction for All Students* builds on that work and extends the study of teaching and learning to include differentiation of instruction, 21st century thinking skills, and collegial collaboration.

Orchestrating A Positive Learning-Centered Environment

Positive Learning- Centered Environment

Developing Thinking Skills for the 21st Century
Instruction for All Students Chapter XI, pages 217- 248

Building Appropriate & Positive Personal Relationships with Students
Instruction for All Students pages 6-7,13, 252
Why Didn't I Learn This in College? pages 10-11, 14-15

Additional Resources for Creating a Positive Learning-Centered Environment

- *For Our Students, For Ourselves* video from McCrel
- *The Skillful Teacher* by Jon Saphier and Robert Gower
- *Control Theory in the Classroom* by William Glasser
- *Discipline with Dignity* by Richard Curwin and Allen Mendler
- *Beyond Discipline: From Compliance to Community* by Alfie Kohn
- *People Skills* by Robert Bolton
- *T.E.T.* by Thomas Gordon

Productive Learning-Centered Environment
Ideas to Try... Best Practices to Note... Suggestions...

> *I want to try to... I want/need to be more purposeful about... I/You might consider... I noticed that... I/You need to... It is likely to promote student achievement if I/You ...*

- Use **flexible room arrangements** to match instructional objectives and desired student interaction
- **Identify room arrangements that work best in small group work, whole class discussion, and testing**
- **Teach students to help you arrange/rearrange the student desks/tables quickly and safely**
- Arrange the room so that you can **move around the room with ease**
- **Reduce distance and barriers** between you and your students
- When working with a small group, position yourself so that you can **monitor other students at work**
- **Rotate duties among students** on a scheduled basis
- **Identify needed routines and procedures to ensure maximized learning time**
- **Explain, model, and practice routines and procedures** so that they can be regularly used by students and teacher without need for further explanation
- **Plan and use a short and relevant exercise for students to engage in as they enter the classroom** (These are called sponges, bell ringers, starters, fillers or anchoring activities.)
- **Be sure you have students' attention before beginning instruction or giving directions**
- Use high results attention moves such as **wait time, the look, proximity, and circulation**
- **Provide practice and processing time**
- **Post the agenda and the learning outcomes** on the board, overhead, or chart in the same place each day
- **Explain the work to be done and how to do it**

Planning Instruction

Professionalism & Collegial Collaboration

Implementing Instruction

Organizing a Productive Environment

Assessing Learning & the Instructional Program

Orchestrating a Positive Environment

Productive Learning-Centered Environment
More Ideas to Try... Best Practices to Note... Suggestions...

> *I want to try to... I want/need to be more purposeful about... I/You might consider... I noticed that... I/You need to... It is likely to promote student achievement if I/You ...*

- Check to be sure **students know before they start work what to do and how to do it**

- Repeat and stress complex directions and difficult points; **write out steps to any process having three or more steps**

- **Repeat or rephrase questions and explanations** students do not understand or have students do so for each other

- **Use known or easy content to teach a new process, and use a known process to introduce or teach difficult new material**

- **Assist students in developing organizational systems** that work for them

- Teach students how to use **graphic organizers, mnemonics, and visualizations**

- **Teach students note-taking and reading strategies**

- **Provide opportunities for students to use a variety of learning strategies and to learn which works best for them** so that they can become independent learners

- Build in **movement**

- **Teach students to identify text structure and to use the appropriate graphic organizers** to capture key information

- **Warn students of upcoming transitions**

- **Match the pace of the instruction with the complexity of the concepts being studied and with the amount of unfamiliar vocabulary**

- **Mass practice at the beginning** of new learning and follow-up with **distributed practice throughout the learning**

- After practice of small chunks, **move quickly to meaningful use of the information and skills**

Productive Learning-Centered Environment
More Ideas to Try... Best Practices to Note... Suggestions...

> *I want to try to... I want/need to be more purposeful about... I/You might consider... I noticed that... I/You need to... It is likely to promote student achievement if I/You ...*

- **Write directions for classwork and homework** on board, chart, or transparency

- **Use flexible grouping** determined by such variables as readiness levels, interest, information processing styles, student choice, and, on occasion, random order

- Stay focused on learning; **do not let "off-the-mark" behavior or backtalk take you off track**; notice and deal with it when it fits your agenda.

- **Identify the causes of inattentive or disruptive behavior and match your response to the perceived cause**

- **Wait** to hold discussions about inattentive or disruptive behavior, or unment expectations, **until both of you are calm**

- **Focus on future behavior** rather than on past behavior

- **Include students in developing procedures for handling inappropriate behavior or unmet expectations**

- Use **logical consequences** directly related to the behavior

- Use a **clearly articulated range of consequences** for unmet expectations based on the quality, intensity, and frequency of the action

- **Organize supplies, equipment, and papers** so that they are easily assessable; eliminate clutter

Planning Instruction

Professionalism & Collegial Collaboration

Implementing Instruction

Organizing a Productive Environment

Assessing Learning & the Instructional Program

Orchestrating a Positive Environment

Productive Learning-Centered Environment
Reflections and Questions

> *How might I/you...? How do I/you feel it went when I/you...? Why do I/you think that is so? What did I/you learn from the situation in which I/you...? What does the data/research tell me/you about ...?*

- How do you **involve students in creating and evaluating their own organizational systems?**

- How would you handle/how have you handled **difficult human relations or a communications problem?**

- **What systems do you use to manage time and keep yourself organized?**

- How do you **organize materials and equipment to facilitate learning?**

- What **classroom routines do you use to enhance student time on meaningful tasks?**

- **How well are the routines/procedures you have established working?** What data to you have to support your evaluation of the effectiveness of your routines/procedures?

- How do you **engage students in "ownership" of the classroom** and its smooth operation?

- Describe your **record-keeping procedures-** which ones are working well and which ones are you working to improve?

- **How are you using technology to track student performance?** What do you see as logical next steps in using technology as an organizational tool?

- How do I/you **ensure consistent communication with students, colleagues, parents, and the community?**

- What issues are the focus of your **"mental movies"** when you are rehearsing/reviewing your plans for an upcoming lesson?

- Describe your thinking about **resource allocation to include time, space, materials, and attention** to ensure active and equitable learning for all

ASK Framework for
The Study of Teaching and Learning

The **ASK Framework** is presented here with notations of support materials found in *Leading the Learning* (Rutherford, 2005), *Why Didn't I Learn This in College?* (Rutherford, 2009), and *Instruction for All Students* (Rutherford, 2008).

Planning Instruction

Professionalism

Implementing Instruction

Organizing a Productive Environment

Assessing Learning & the Instructional Program

Orchestrating a Positive Environment

Why Didn't I Learn This in College? is written for novice teachers and their supervisors, mentors, and coaches. The content focuses on planning, instruction, building a learning community, and creating and implementing organizational systems for effective learning in a learning-centered classroom. *Instruction for All Students* builds on that work and extends the study of teaching and learning to include differentiation of instruction, 21st century thinking skills, and collegial collaboration.

Organizing & Leading a
Productive Learning-Centered Environment

Creating and Using Organizational Systems for Professional and Instructional Materials
   Instruction for All Students pages 262-266
   Why Didn't I Learn This in College? pages 193-220

Developing and Implementing Organizational Systems for Learners and the Classroom (Space, Time, Procedures, Transitions, Gaining Attention)
   Instruction for All Students pages 262-266
   Why Didn't I Learn This in College? pages 221-254

Proactively Addressing the Needs of Reluctant and Resistant Learners
   Instruction for All Students pages 251, 258-261
   Why Didn't I Learn This in College? pages 32-44

Additional Resources on Creating
A Productive Learning-Centered Environment

- *The Skillful Teacher* by Jon Saphier and Robert Gower
- *What to Do With the Kid Who...* by Kay Burke
- *Discipline with Dignity* by Richard Curwin and Allen Mendler

Professionalism and Collegial Collaboration
Ideas to Try... Best Practices to Note... Suggestions...

> *I want to try to... I want/need to be more purposeful about... I/You might consider... I noticed that... I/You need to... It is likely to promote student achievement if I/You ...*

- Use the **district mission and vision statements, the district learning standards, and the criteria for professional performance as benchmarks** for professional practice

- Demonstrate knowledge about and use of **current state and federal laws** regarding special services students

- **Consult with and inform appropriate personnel around legal questions**

- **Keep your grade book updated and legible**

- **Maintain accurate attendance records**

- **Inventory** school property, books, and instructional materials and **maintain accurate records**

- **Perform duties** such as restroom supervision, lunch duty, hall duty, and bus duty as assigned

- **Use clear, concise, and grammatically correct language in oral and written communication**

- **Submit reports correctly and on time**

- **Attend required meetings**

- **Be prompt to and attentive at staff, departmental, and team meetings**

- **Participate and contribute at staff, departmental, and team meetings**

- **Provide substitute with thorough instructional plans** and notes on classroom procedures

- **Develop and make accessible emergency substitute plans**

- **Handle situations involving staff members in a professional manner**

- **Implement decisions made by groups** in which teacher served or was represented

Planning Instruction

Professionalism & Collegial Collaboration

Implementing Instruction

Organizing a Productive Environment

Assessing Learning & the Instructional Program

Orchestrating a Positive Environment

Professionalism & Collegial Collaboration
More Ideas to Try... Best Practices to Note...

> *I want to try to... I want/need to be more purposeful about... I/You might consider... I noticed that... I/You need to... It is likely to promote student achievement if I/You ...*

- **Maintain Internet access safeguards** appropriate to age level and as identified by the district
- **Use discretion in handling confidential information and difficult situations**
- **Ensure that supportable facts,** rather than rumors or insinuations, **are discussion points in conversations and conferences**
- **Be available for conferences with parents**
- **Seek out parents** and make parents feel comfortable contacting you and interacting with you **as a partner in their child's education**
- **Teach parents** about the instructional program and your approach to learning through newsletters and evening academic events that feature student work and expected standards
- **Collaborate with special education teachers/general education teachers** to facilitate the learning of students with IEPs
- **Seek out and use professional expertise** for assistance and guidance in supporting students with intellectual, emotional, or physical challenges
- **Serve as a school representative** when asked to do so
- **Serve as a catalyst for constructive change**
- Demonstrate responsibility in **attendance and punctuality** as required by school policy
- Always be **professionally groomed and attired**
- **Express views and ideas to others in a professional manner** that is respectful of the possibility and probability of different perspectives

Professionalism & Collegial Collaboration
More Ideas to Try... Best Practices to Note...

> *I want to try to... I want/need to be more purposeful about... I/You might consider... I noticed that... I/You need to... It is likely to promote student achievement if I/You ...*

- **Align professional development work with school and district goals**
- **Adjust classroom practice as a result of professional learning** completed independently, in collaboration with colleagues, and/or sponsored by the school or district
- **Work with colleagues across grade levels to align curriculum and decrease redundancy**
- **Recognize that collegial sharing is essential to the learning process** for both students and educators
- **Use all available resources** accessible locally, at the state level, nationally, and technologically
- **Use communication skills that demonstrate an awareness of cultural, gender, and generational differences**
- **Assess group dynamics and productivity and adjust own behavior to maximize the outcomes of the work**

Professionalism & Collegial Collaboration
Reflections and Questions

> *How might I/you...? How do I/you feel it went when I/you...? Why do I/you think that is so? What did I/you learn from the situation in which I/you...? What does the data/research tell me/you about ...?*

- Describe ways that you have **shared new ideas and your expertise with colleagues**

- Describe your efforts to **foster collegial collaboration among school staff**

- How do you **initiate/create opportunities to be a resource** to other teachers?

- How have you **contributed to the development and implementation of district, school, department or team programs and goals?**

- Describe the **professional development opportunities in which you have been engaged**; explain how and why you chose those particular professional development activities

- **How have you integrated what you have learned** through participation in professional development opportunities into your practice in ways that impacted student learning and achievement?

- What opportunities have you sought to **mentor a colleague**, whether a new teacher or a teacher attempting to learn a new technique or area of content?

- How do you use **school-based specialists, district personnel and resources, and professional organizations** to support student achievement?

- How do you **coordinate your efforts** with other staff members?

- How do you keep abreast of **new developments in your field?**

- Describe your own **collaboration and co-teaching involvement?**

- How does your lesson and unit design process reflect the **beliefs, vision, and mission of the district?**

- What opportunities exist for **community members to view student work and provide feedback?**

- Describe how your practice demonstrates your belief that **all the students belong to all of us**

Professionalism & Collegial Collaboration
Reflections and Questions

How might I/you…? How do I/ you feel it went when I/you…? Why do I/you think that is so? What did I/you learn from the situation in which I/you…? What does the data/research tell me/you about …?

- Describe **instructional materials you have designed/developed** yourself or in collaboration with others; describe the process you used in development

- Describe how you have **sought out grant programs** to enhance your instructional program

- Describe situations in which you have **piloted materials/programs**; what did you learn from that process?

- Describe the ways you are involved with **student activities as a spectator, active supporter, sponsor, or initiator**

- What are the ways that you ensure that **parent partnership** goes beyond volunteering and includes decision-making?

Framework for
The Study of Teaching and Learning

The **ASK Framework** is presented here with notations of support materials found in *Leading the Learning* (Rutherford, 2005), *Why Didn't I Learn This in College?* (Rutherford, 2009), and *Instruction for All Students* (Rutherford, 2008).

Why Didn't I Learn This in College? is written for novice teachers and their supervisors, mentors, and coaches. The content focuses on planning, instruction, building a learning community, and creating and implementing organizational systems for effective learning in a learning-centered classroom. *Instruction for All Students* builds on that work and extends the study of teaching and learning to include differentiation of instruction, 21st century thinking skills, and collegial collaboration.

Professionalism and Collegial Collaboration

See *Leading the Learning* pages 122-126 for ideas to try, best practices to note, suggestions to make, questions to ask, and related resources.

The Ways We Collaborate: Consultant, Collaborator, and Coach
Leading the Learning pages 190-198

Formats for Collaboration and Job Embedded Learning
Leading the Learning pages 11-61
Instruction for All Students Chapter XI, pages 267-291

Peer Observation
Leading the Learning pages 39-40
Instruction for All Students pages 275-279

Mentoring
Leading the Learning pages 51-55
Instruction for All Students pages 290-291

Co-Teaching
Instruction for All Students pages 286-289

Professional Responsibilities
Why Didn't I Learn This in College? pages 195-220

Parents as Partners
Why Didn't I Learn This in College? Chapter X, pages 259-272

Additional Resources for
Professionalism and
Collegial Collaboration

- *Results Driven Professional Development* by St. Vrain Valley Office of Professional Development
- *Cognitive Coaching* by Art Costa and Bob Garmstron
- *Mentoring Matters* by Laura Lipton and Bruce Wellman

Professionalism & Collegial Collaboration

Planning Instruction

Implementing Instruction

Organizing a Productive Environment

Assessing Learning & the Instructional Program

Orchestrating a Positive Environment

Leading
the
Learning

Using Multiple Methods of
Data Collection

Multiple Methods
of
Data Collection

This section provides support for teachers, mentors, coaches, and supervisors in their efforts to use multiple sources of data to inform their teaching, mentoring, coaching, and supervisory practice in the interest of student learning. The essential questions addressed are:

- What are potential sources of data to use in building a body of evidence about the results of the teaching and leading decisions we make and the actions we take?

- What data do we already have available and how might we use it in supervising, mentoring, and coaching?

- What are the ways in which we can look beyond teacher work to include student work as a part of our data?

Potential Sources of Data

Just as teachers gather assessment data in many ways, supervisors and coaches gather data about the work and the impact of teacher work on student learning in a variety of ways. **The use of multiple data sources helps ALL of us adjust our practice to enhance the learning of those we are teaching and leading.** To that end, it is recommended that supervision and evaluation processes include an acknowledgement that data sources about teacher work go well beyond traditional formal observations. That formal observations, while important, provide a limited picture of the complexity of teacher work.

Listed below are some, but certainly not all, possible sources of data about areas of professional performance. Some are useful with all areas while others are useful in selected areas. Those marked with an asterisk (*) are data sources that are already in place for other purposes but that have not, in the past, been officially acknowledged as data sources in the supervision and evaluation process.

- **Formal observation process**
- **Planning conferences**
- **Informal observations**
  - ►walk-throughs
  - ►parent/teacher conferences
  - ►professional development events
  - ►professional meetings
- **Student work***
- **Student achievement data***
  - ►state*
  - ►district*
  - ►classroom assessments*
  - ►longitudinal rubrics
  - ►grade distribution reports*
- **Journals**
- **Self-Assessment**
- **Annual or multi-year professional goal/growth statements with action plans and documented results***
- **Teacher work**
  - ► year, unit, and daily lesson plans*
  - ► action research
  - ► review of records, such as plan book, grade book, teacher-prepared materials, grading policy*

Potential Sources of Data

- ➤ teacher logs/records of after school assistance provided to students
- ➤ substitute plans*
- ➤ teacher's parent conference notes, phone logs*
- ➤ written communication initiated by the teacher, such as notes, memos, letters, and newsletters to parents, students, and colleagues*
- ➤ documentation of involvement in school and professional activities*

- **Portfolios**

- **Documentation of efforts/accomplishments in teacher leadership roles, such as mentor, department chair, team leader, curriculum design, professional development facilitator/coach, instructional advisory board, and program coordinator (i.e., International Baccalaureate, Reading Recovery)**

- **Shadowing**

- **Conversations and conferences**
  - ➤ planning conferences
  - ➤ reflective conferences
  - ➤ conversations*
  - ➤ structured interviews
  - ➤ book clubs
  - ➤ study groups
  - ➤ team meetings
  - ➤ department meetings
  - staff meetings

- **Transcripts or certificates of participation in professional development***

- **Feedback from students, parents, colleagues, and community**
  - ➤ written communications about the teacher, such as letters from parents, citations from organizations, and memos from school system personnel*
  - ➤ feedback from parent and counselor conferences
  - ➤ feedback from volunteers and business/community resources
  - ➤ substitute reports
  - ➤ student or parent surveys

- **School data sources**
  - ➤ pattern of discipline referrals and follow-up*
  - ➤ required reports for school and district*
  - ➤ requests for student placement, such as student requests to be placed in or taken out of the class or teacher requests for student to be removed*
  - ➤ attendance records*

Data Sources by Areas of Performance

Planning Instruction:
Essential understandings/questions
Pacing guide/calendar
Unit plans
Lesson plans
Individual curriculum maps
Grade level, team, or subject area curriculum maps
Assessment plan
Student Achievement Plan
Substitute plans
Conferences

Assessing Learning and the Instructional Program:
Assessment plan
Assessments
Grading plan
Grade book
Student work samples
Student achievement data
Formal observations
Informal observations
Conversations
Conferences
Rubrics

Implementing Instruction:
Unit review
Extension/enrichment activities
Review/reinforcement activities
Differentiation/modifications
Flexible group plans
Student work samples
Homework assignments and guides
Videos, audiotapes, or photographs of
        instruction/students at work
Formal observations
Informal observations
Feedback from students, parents, and colleagues

Data Sources by Areas of Performance

Positive Learning Environment:
Formal observations
Informal observations
Conferences and conversations
Feedback from students, parents, and colleagues

Productive Learning Environment:
Formal observations
Informal observations
Conferences and conversations
Student achievement data
Student work

Professionalism:
Teacher artifacts
Informal observations
Records review
Feedback from students, parents and colleagues
Interactions with community
Parent conferences
Parent communications
Journals/logs
Conversations
Professional involvement
Team meetings
Department meetings
Faculty meetings

St. Vrain Valley School District's
Areas of Professional Performance Data Log

Teacher _____   Assignment _____

Supervisor _____   Year _____

I. Plans Curriculum, Instruction, & Assessment

A. Uses District Standards and the standards-based planning process to plan for the year, units, and daily lessons

Data/Source

- Curriculum map for year is based on standards (Source: curriculum maps)
- Uses graphic organizers to backward design units (Source: teacher plans and conversations)
- Shared copy of course outline given to students, which identifies essential learnings
- Course syllabus exhibits flow of learning across the standards
- Posted agenda leads to conversations around learning goals for the unit and the day (Source: walk-throughs)

B. Uses District standards and outcomes, designs sequential units of study that make learning cumulative and connects learning across disciplines

Data/Source

- Observable and recorded scores/data on literacy and math tasks in other content areas
- Uses school-wide writing rubric
- Social studies teacher incorporating math into social studies curriculum (Source: request for materials)
- Uses common assessment addressing standards across the curriculum (Source: team meeting discussions, data sheets, student work)

C. Is knowledgeable about the content to be taught and uses that knowledge to design assessment and instruction around essential understandings

Data/Source

- Uses curriculum map based on standards to plan for the year
- Documents and communicates expectations and essential learnings (Source: artifacts to include lesson plans and copies of assessments plus walk-throughs)
- Distributes both course and unit essential questions to students in fall and refers to them daily (Source: teacher handout, posted in classroom as seen during walk-throughs)
- Shares content knowledge and best practice pedagogy with staff (Source: observation of staff workshops)

D. Uses knowledge of human development and learning theory to plan instruction

Data/Source

- Uses information from readings on brain research to design unit (Source: conversations and journal entries, student work, menus)
- Uses knowledge learned in book club on Marzano's book (Source: walk-through, conversations, student work)
- Reflects on implications of information learned through books, articles, and workshops (Source: conversations)
- Assesses prior knowledge, surface misconceptions, and promotes student processing by using 10:2 Theory (Source: multiple walk-throughs)
- Uses developmentally appropriate manipulatives and tools (Source: walk-throughs)

E. Assesses student differences in performance levels, learning styles, cultural heritage, language, socio-economic backgrounds, and physical and emotional disabilities to plan appropriate learning experiences

Data/Source

- Uses flow chart showing student performance on CSAP, Terra Nova, and classroom assessments (Source: flow chart and explanation of use)
- Uses knowledge of language acquisition and structure of language to plan/create visual organizers to scaffold instruction (Source: student work and forms)
- Analyzes and uses literacy data...SRI, SOAR, Gates-M, STAR, common course/department assessments (Source: department meeting discussions)
- Uses literacy data to create flexible groups (Source: IRI, HM, theme tests, HM benchmarks, HM baseline data, running records, teacher observations, CSAP scores)
- Reviews IEP's and discusses ways to modify instruction to meet individual needs (Source: IEP's, discussions, and lesson plans)
- Uses Multiple Intelligences in planning (Source: student interviews)
- Uses reteaching as well as enrichment opportunities (Source: teacher artifacts, student interviews, student work, anecdotal notes)

F. Selects and/or designs and uses a variety of assessments aligned to instructional objectives and the district standards

Data/Source

- Uses a balance of traditional and performance assessments (Source: actual assessments and student work)
- Designs performance assessments that are coherent, valid, authentic, and rigorous (Source: teacher analysis of assessments using a rubric for performance assessments)
- Uses formative assessments to help students self-assess and to provide rehearsals for summative assessments (Source: student portfolios, teacher portfolios)
- Graphs results of different assessments and talks about similarities and differences found in the results (Source: teacher artifacts)

G. Task analyzes to identify necessary knowledge, skills, and levels of thinking required for successful learning, and then plans for multiple pathways to learning

Data/Source

- Uses grids analyzing specific tasks and what is required for each (Source: observations, plans)
- Uses flexible grouping (Source: plans, walk-throughs, observations)
- Differentiates through reading groups, tutoring, and focus groups (Source: walk-throughs)
- Uses menus, centers, and choices for assessments (Source: artifacts, walk-throughs)
- Consults with Literacy Lab/Media staff around obtaining materials at various reading levels: provides cart of "choices materials" in classroom (Source: conversations, photos, walk-throughs)

II. Implementing Instruction
A. Actively engages students in learning experiences that access prior knowledge, requires varied and complex thinking skills, and provides real world connections

Data/Source

- One page compare/contrast paper (Source: walk-throughs)
- Small reading groups (text to self, text to text, text to word) (Source: charts, means observations, conversations, lesson plans)
- Uses KWL, consensogram, Venn diagrams
- Consistent attempts to pre-assess to determine prior knowledge (Source: daily plans, walk-throughs, observation of instruction, video of lessons)
- Integrates content into literature and math (Source: charts, menus, observations, walk-throughs, conversations)
- Interest inventories and pretests (Source: documents)
- Use of flexible grouping based on student readiness and interests (Source: observations, discussions)
- Analysis of unit and lesson plans (Source: discussion)
- Offers choice about learning approaches or assessments (Source: plans, final student work)
- Students/teachers discussing connection to student's real world (Source: student writing, product)

B. Continually uses formative assessment data to inform instructional practice

Data/Source

- Writing samples - teacher and student track growth
- Theme tests
- Pre/post testing
- Reading groups (Source: anecdotal notes, IRIs)
- Teacher tracks growth data throughout the year (Source: spreadsheets, grading practices, team meeting discussions)

C. Integrates literacy, numeracy, and available technology across the curriculum

Data/Source

- Reading strategies taught during all subjects (Source: curriculum maps, plans, conversations, lesson observations, expository text)
- Writing in math to explain answers
- Rubrics include both literacy/numeracy objectives (Source: projects)
- Writing required to explain thinking (Source: unit plans, conversations)
- Reading and math objectives are evident throughout the day (Source: expository text, walk-throughs, rubrics, posters)
- Rubrics include both literacy and numeracy
- Teacher explicitly identifies/models/practices multiple strategies to solve problem (Source: posted strategies, observation, student artifacts)
- Teacher uses PowerPoint to instruct students (Source: student work/observations)
- IBM e-mentors are used
- Students create multi-media projects in lab
- Students complete research
- Explicit identification of modeling, practicing multiple strategies to solve a problem (a bank), labels them (Source: posted strategies, classroom observations, student work)

D. Communicates the learning standards, related learning experiences, assessment methods and criteria in age appropriate language, and provides models of learning processes and exemplars of products

Data/Source

- Teacher models assignment for students
- Sample materials to use for reference
- Teacher refers to posted standards in relation to daily agenda
- Shared writing (to, with, by) modeling thinking process
- Anchor papers shown to students (Source: walk-throughs)
- Student use of standards-based instructional rubrics (Source: rubrics in student language)
- Instructional planning targets specific standards (Source: lesson plan)
- Models of student work that targets standards posted in the classroom (Source: examples of student work)
- Teacher aligns assessment with instruction and uses a variety of assessments (Source: examples of assessments)
- Posted standards and expectations (Source: documents)
- Handouts, packet explaining assessment (Source: documents)
- Posted standards that are mentioned through class
- Students using rubrics (Source: rubrics in student language)
- Instructional planning targets students (Source: curriculum maps, lesson plans)
- Student work targeting students (Source: student work displayed in classroom)

The Formal Observation Process

The formal observation process usually includes a pre-observation conference, an observation of at least thirty minutes, a post-observation, and a written report. In most districts teachers "in the cycle" are observed two to three times a year and each observer has fifteen to thirty teachers to observe. The majority of supervision and evaluation systems are structured so that novice teachers are observed during each of the first three years and veteran teachers every three or four years.

The evolution of best practice in classroom assessment has led to assessment being integrated into instruction rather than being something that is done at the end of instruction and into being used as data to inform instructional decisions. It makes sense that assessment of teacher performance should become more integrated into the fabric of school life rather than being the event it is currently perceived to be. It also should be used to inform supervisors about their instructional leadership decisions around individual teachers and the entire staff.

This rethinking the role of the formal observation process is not about "out with the old and in with the new." It is about developing a repertoire of data gathering tools and using each appropriately and well. Just as formal, read that traditional, paper and pencil assessment continues to be an important component of the classroom teacher's assessment repertoire, as should the components of the formal observation process. Care should be taken to develop skills at observing and analyzing teaching and learning, writing reports, and holding conferences with teachers to discuss the observation and to, **make suggestions, give directions, or ask questions in such a way as to promote teacher growth**.

Unfortunately in the minds of educators, this process, as it is currently implemented, often creates negative feelings. Observers bemoan the **time** it takes to complete the various components of the process, including the hours spent at the computer writing "**The Report**." The teachers being observed often perceive the observation as, and even call it, "an evaluation." This means they spend hours in preparation for the observation and plan lessons that are often not representative of their everyday practice. In the worst case scenario teachers and students rehearse the lesson to be observed to ensure that the teacher is seen as competent during the observation. For example, one teacher related that he told students to raise their hands to answer all questions even if they did not know the answer. He further instructed them to raise their right hand if they knew the answer and to raise their left hands if they did not know the answer. He told them that he would only call on those who had raised their right hands. Even more depressing is the teacher who told colleagues that she had wasted a great lesson that morning. When asked why it was wasted she replied that she spent hours planning it and

The Formal Observation Process

then the supervisor was unable to complete the observation. To compound the problem, rather than looking forward to a professional dialogue about the shared teaching and learning experience, teachers are anxious to see if the observer saw the performance as competent and reads **"The Report"** mainly to see if the observer liked what was seen in the classroom. We clearly need to reexamine our practice if we hold professional growth and student learning as goals of the supervision and evaluation process,

Few observers or teachers feel that the time and energy invested in the formal observation process provides anywhere near the opportunities for professional growth that face-to-face interactions with each other and colleagues provide. The irony is that the reason most often cited by supervisors for not having those frequent face-to-face professional interactions is the time that must be spent on the formal observation process. Given that, we must work to ensure that when contracts call for the use of the formal observation process, and when the situation warrants it as the data gathering source of choice, we are knowledgeable and skillful in our use of the process.

Planning and Reflective Conferences

Guidelines for pre-conferences that are called planning conferences in this book and for post-conferences that are called reflective conferences in this book are found on pages 144-146, 193-195 and in **Tool-15: Providing Context for Formal Observation**. The name changes are meant to reflect what actually occurs at each of these conferences and to indicate that each component can stand alone. That is, a planning conference can be held without being followed by an observation and a reflective conference can occur without being proceeded by an observation. In fact, the case is made that such practice can be both time efficient and growth inducing.

The Formal Observation Process
Observations

A formal observation is a classroom visitation by the supervisor, mentor, or coach lasting at least 30 uninterrupted minutes. During this observation, the observer gathers data by observing the teacher and the learners, by looking at teaching and learning artifacts, and by interacting with students in an unobtrusive way.

This type of observation is often preceded by a planning conference during which the planning process and lesson outcomes are discussed. A planning conference is highly recommended because both parties can grow professionally from it, and the results of this time intensive process can be maximized as a professional development opportunity. In any event, the planning process and lesson outcomes should be shared prior to the formal observation so that the supervisor, mentor, or coach knows the context in which the events in the classroom are occurring.

In order to capture and later analyze the important events and patterns, the observer needs to take notes. Notes should reflect not only teacher actions and words, but also focus on the words and actions of students, as well as information about the classroom environment. Data gathered is analyzed and recorded in a written observation report and shared at a reflective conference. Some current contracts may require that the report may be written before the reflective conference. Given a goal of developing reflective practitioners and the value placed on face-to-face interaction, it is strongly recommended that the report be finalized following the conference and include discussion points and decisions made at the reflective conference.

In the vernacular of the profession this type observation is often referred to as an "evaluation." As clearly articulated in documents from Barrington Community Unit School District 220, Barrington, Illinois, this observation is not synonymous with the evaluation process because it is only one component of that process. Be careful with your own word choice and clarify as often as necessary the role of observations in the supervision and evaluation process. Until this distinction is understood by all parties, teacher growth resulting from the formal observation process will be minimal. When the formal observation process is combined with or replaced by frequent informal observations and when mentors and coaches are doing frequent classroom observations, the notion that observations are evaluation is diminished.

The Formal Observation Process
Observations

To Establish Context

In order to make the formal observation process an opportunity for teacher growth and to maximize the understanding of the observer care must be taken to establish context for the teaching and learning episode to be observed. Artifacts to review include:

- the lesson plan
- the standards of learning to be addressed
- student achievement data
- discipline referrals
- past observation reports and evaluations
- professional growth plans
- professional development plans

When formal observations are combined with walk-throughs and other data gathering methods, the context is already established and such a structured review is not necessary. If, however, the formal observations are the only times the supervisor is in the classroom observing and interacting with the students, the process becomes one of jumping through the contractual hoops.

Note Taking Tips

Given the focus on looking at student work and student achievement data gathering practices need to be extended beyond recording what the teacher says and does. While is it important to capture significant teacher actions, it is perhaps even more important to observe and capture the essence of what happens after the teacher stops talking. Teachers often complain that supervisors miss what is going on because they are so busy writing. Be sure to look at student work, interview students, observe posted student work, and make note of the data you gather.

Whatever formula is used to decide how much to write, it is critical to avoid checklists. Paper with only the teacher's name, the date, and any areas of focus is the best approach. Laptop computers may be efficient for quickly gathering data and translating that data into an observation report, but the use of one during formal observations may greatly decrease interaction with students and the focus on student learning.

One technique that many supervisors have found useful is to take notes on stick-on notes. When preparing for the reflective conference or for writing the observation report, the stick-on notes are easily sorted into the standards or domains that structure the performance criteria.

The Formal Observation Process
Observations

Focused or Comprehensive Observations

As a teacher moves through the evaluation cycle, the supervisor, mentor, or coach should be able to document not only student learning but teacher growth. There is power in having teachers identify the areas where they need to focus their growth and, therefore, the feedback. This does not mean, however, that the supervisor, mentor, or coach cannot do comprehensive observations or have other areas of focus. It simply means that the observer is contracting to give the teacher data or feedback on the requested areas.

Over the period of an evaluation cycle all performance criteria that are observable in the classroom should be examined and noted. If the formal observation process is the only recognized data source, supervisors need to review the performance criteria and past observation reports before subsequent observations. Missing data can be targeted as the observation focus to ensure that when it is time to write the summative evaluation report, they have a complete and accurate picture of teacher decision making and performance.

In order to keep the data gathering process from becoming overwhelming, consider data already gathered. For example, there may be a body of evidence that the teacher is accomplished with the use of time and space and has smoothly functioning organizational systems in place. Once that is clearly established there is no need to continue to take notes about or write about this area of performance. There are so many other areas of professional practice on which to focus that is a waste of time to continue to focus on management and organizational issues.

Do not lose sight of the focus on student learning. It is important to not be overly impressed by students "on task" without checking to see if the task was worth doing. While orderly classrooms are essential to learning, it is also important to note that control and compliance are not synonymous with student learning. **One way to maintain a focus on student learning is to target students on whom to concentrate.** Select students who are high achievers and struggling or resistant learners. Be sure to notice how they respond to and interact with the teacher and classmates. Also note how the teacher seeks out, responds to, and interacts with these students. Targeting students in this way will enrich the quality of the data you gather.

Planning Conferences

Planning conferences provide opportunities to gather data, establish context, and interact as a coach, collaborator, or consultant. If the intent of the supervision process is teacher growth and student learning, the time spent in this meeting provides a tremendous opportunity for the supervisor, mentor, or coach to be an instructional leader. The planning conference provides the ultimate **"teachable moment."** It is hard to imagine a better time to help a teacher shape his or her own thinking or to learn more about instructional decision- making.

While there is certainly a need for "unannounced" informal observations, and perhaps even formal observations, planning conferences prior to formal observations are an important part of our repertoire for professional interactions. In team teaching and co-teaching situations consider having both teachers participate in the planning conference so that their professional interactions can be considered as a component of the supervisory process, as well as provide additional learning opportunities for all. Planning conferences also can be held when there is no intention of following up with an observation. The sole purpose, in this instance, can be simply to plan a lesson, unit, or map out a semester or course. These conferences may include small groups or teams rather than being one-on-one interactions.

Planning Conferences Prior to a Formal Observation

Essential understandings for an observer prior to a formal observation are:
- What students are supposed to know and be able to do as a result of the learning experiences to be observed
- How those outcomes relate to district standards, benchmarks, and indicators
- How student learning will be assessed in both formative and summative ways
- How the learning experiences in which the students will be engaged are related to what they are supposed to learn, to prior lessons, and to the big picture of the unit and the year
- The sequence of the lesson
- How data has been used to determine the best course of action
- What learning difficulties have been and are expected to be encountered and the plans for dealing with those problems
- Any other contextual information
- Any special areas of focus, as well as rationale for that focus, as identified by the supervisor, coach, or mentor or by the teacher

"The Top Ten Questions to Focus Discussions of the Teaching and Learning Process" on the next page provide discussion starting points for planning conferences.

TOP TEN QUESTIONS
to Focus Discussions
of the Teaching and Learning Process

1. What should **students know and be able to do** as a result of this lesson? How are these objectives related to national, state, and/or **district standards?**

2. How do **students demonstrate what they know and what they can do** with what they know? Are there multiple forms of assessment including student **self-assessment?** What is the **assessment criteria** and what form does it take?

3. How do you plan to **find out** what **students already know (preassessment)** and help them access what they know and have experienced both inside and outside the classroom? How do the learners not only **build on prior experiences** but **reframe their thinking** when appropriate?

4. How are new knowledge, concepts, and skills to be introduced? Given the **diversity of the students** and the **task analysis,** what **options for sources of information and presentation modes** are used?

5. How do students **process (make meaning of) their learning?** What key questions, activities, and assignments (in class or homework) promote retention, understanding and transfer?

6. What are the **formative assessments** or **checks for student understanding** during the lesson? How is data from those assessments used to inform teaching decisions?

7. How is **instruction differentiated** so that the learning experiences are productive for all students? Are students encouraged to **process** and **demonstrate learning** in different ways?

8. How is the learning framed **so that students know the objectives,** the **rationale** for the objectives and activities, the directions and procedures, the **assessment task and criteria,** as well the connection of the lesson and the activities to the standards and to life beyond the classroom.

9. How are opportunities for students to make **real world connections** and to learn and use the **varied and complex thinking skills** built into the learning experiences?

10. What adjustments are made in the **learning environment** and in **instruction** so that all students can work and learn efficiently? How is **data** used to make these decisions?

Planning Conferences

Marcia Baldanza, Principal of Patrick Henry Elementary School, Alexandria City Public Schools, Alexandria, Virginia, has created two menus of questions to use in planning conferences; she chooses the menu based on the attitudes, skills, and knowledge of the teacher with whom she is conferencing.

Planning Conference A (Global and Contextual)

- What is it you want students to know and be able to do as a result of the lesson today?
- How is this related to the Virginia Standards of Learning and school priorities?
- Where are you and the learners in this unit of study?
- What kinds of relevant and important learning experiences have occurred during the past few weeks in your class?
- How do you intend to follow up on those experiences in the coming weeks?
- What activities will you have students engaged in during this lesson?
- Why did you select these activities for use at this time?
- Do you want me to observe for anything specific?

Planning Conference B (Specific and Analytical)

- What do you expect students to learn from this lesson?
- As you currently see this lesson, what will be the sequence of events?
- Do you plan to use the text? In addition to the text, what materials or resources will you use to present the concepts and have students process their learning?
- How will you determine whether or not your students have learned what you want them to have learned during the lesson? At the conclusion of the unit study?
- When will transitions from whole group to small group work occur?
- How will movement be built into the learning activities?
- As you see the lesson unfolding, what exactly will students be doing?
- What do you see yourself doing to make this happen? Do you envision any problems or confusions?
- Given that this class period is _____ minutes, how will you chunk the time?
- Are there any special circumstances in the classroom that affect learning or the learning environment? What do you do to accommodate these circumstances?
- Do any particular students or group of students within this class present special challenges? How are you dealing with them?
- Is there anything you have been working on that you would like specific feedback about?

Informal Observations

Performance criteria for most districts includes a standard or domain relating to professionalism and collaboration. In the past, paper documentation has been the most widely used source of data. Informal observations of these events may provide a more accurate picture and certainly provide a far greater opportunity for professional development and teacher growth. While teaching and learning during the school day is the primary focus of the work, teachers deserve both recognition for and feedback on the work they do beyond the classroom.

Parent Teacher Conferences

These conferences are an excellent opportunity to gather data about the relationships that teachers have established with parents, how well they know their students, their skills at communicating student learning, and their belief systems about schooling, students, and the role of parents. Observations of counselors, social workers, and psychologists in parent conferences is a strong data source for the work of those professionals. In these conferences, care must be taken in dealing with issues of confidentiality.

Staffings for Special Education

Observations of these meetings are important sources of data about the decision making and performance of special educators, counselors, social workers, and psychologists. With inclusion and co-teaching the norm, general education teachers also spend a significant amount of time preparing for and participating in these meetings. Data gathered here would include knowledge of law and regulations, instructional strategies that have been tried, collaboration, and communication skills.

Back-to-School Night

These events provide one of the most important public examinations of our practice. Informal observations of teachers during these classroom visits by parents provides data around how teachers present their instructional program in the context of district and school philosophies and initiatives.

Co-Curricular Activities and Coaching

While academic achievement and learning is the primary goal of schooling, the teaching staff supports not only the academic growth of students but also contributes to their affective, social, and physical growth. This work often occurs outside the classroom in club meetings, auditoriums, and on playing fields. Many of the indicators found in professional performance criteria are demonstrated in these settings and should be noted in evaluation reports.

Informal Observations
Walk-Throughs

Walk-throughs are informal brief classroom visitations that may be used for generic data gathering or focused on particular teaching and learning behaviors.

Several education researchers and consultants have written about and advocated the use of these brief and more frequent classroom visits or observations. **Madeline Hunter** talked about conducting classroom observations using a 5 x 5 schedule. She suggested that supervisors could spend thirty minutes visiting five classrooms for five minutes each and thereby greatly increase the frequency of their classroom observations. **Dr. Carolyn Downey** of San Diego State University and **Dr. Lauren Resnick**, Director of the Learning Research and Development Center at the University of Pittsburgh, have focused their work around the power of increasing the frequency of classroom observations by supervisors. Dr. Resnick's efforts have been focused on various stakeholders participating in **Learning Walks** to look for conditions that would promote student achievement of high standards while Dr. Downey has focused on walk-throughs as a component of data gathering in the supervision and evaluation process. **The New Teacher Center**, at the University of California, Santa Cruz calls the short but frequent observations **Quick Visits** in its training program for mentors.

What to Notice During Walk-Throughs: The Experts Say ...
Ellen Muir, Executive Director, and the staff at the New Teacher Center suggest that the focus of the **Quick Visit** should be as follows:
- **Content:** What are the students learning?
- **Strategies:** How are they learning/practicing/applying skills, knowledge and concepts?
- **Alignment:** How does this learning correlate to district standards and to the needs of the students?
  How does this work help students meet performance standards?
  How have student needs been assessed?
  Does the pacing match student needs?
  How is instruction differentiated?

Dr. Resnick recommends that observers:
- Look at the work in which students are engaged
- Examine student work that is displayed in the classroom
- Talk to students
- Talk with the teacher

Walk-Throughs

What to Notice: Identify Your Own "Short List" of Look Fors

Greece Central School District, Greece, New York, has identified six **Attributes of Successful Learning Environments** that are expected to be in place in each classroom. Frequent walk-throughs by teams of district administrators and school administrators helped the leadership reach consensus across a large district about what the attributes look like in practice and served as a stimulus for extensive dialogue with all staff.

Attributes of
Successful Learning Environments
Greece Central School District

- **Teach to New York State Learning Standards and District Outcomes**
- **Emphasize Prior Learning**
- **Apply Knowledge in a Real Life Context**
- **Provide Opportunity for Dialogue and Debate**
- **Provide Ongoing Opportunities (Using a Variety of Strategies) to Assess Student Learning**
- **Promote Rigor in Student Work**

What to Notice: Conversations with Students

Given that our focus is on student learning, it seems important to include looking at student work, watching students at work, observing student/teacher interactions, and asking students questions about their work in the walk-through process. Questions to pose to students include:

- **What are you supposed to be learning?**
- **How is what you are doing helping you learn that?**
- **How will you and your teacher measure your success?**
- **How are you doing in the learning journey?**
- **What are the next steps for you?**
- **How do you know what excellent work looks like?**
- **In what ways do you do self-assessment of your efforts and your work?**

Walk-Throughs

What to Notice: Looking at Student Work

Another area of focus for walk-throughs could be around the kind of work students are doing at the time of the walk-through. Data collected could include:
- Type of task (notetaking, reading, collaborating, listening, etc.)
- Knowledge students were expected to master or demonstrate in the task
- Skills students were expected to be using or demonstrate mastery of
- Level of thinking required of the students in completing the task

See **Tools Section** for a form on which to note observations about student work.

What to Notice: Using District Performance Criteria as the Focus

See the **Areas of Performance Sections** on **Instruction** and **Environment** for a multitude of variables on which to focus during walk-throughs. Short classroom visits might focus on:
- A complete set of criteria as identified by the district, the induction program, or a professional development program
- One or two areas of focus as selected by the district, the observer, the teacher, or a combination thereof
- One or two variables across all the classrooms in the school/district
- An action research project
- Strategies the staff is studying in book clubs or study groups
- Alignment and consistency across teachers and/or buildings

See the **Literacy Walk-Through** developed by Sharon Edwards and Jacalyn Colt of St. Vrain Valley School District, Longmont, Colorado on page 153.

What to Notice: A Collaborative Approach

Use the Graffiti technique described on page 21 to have staff generate lists of look-fors or to further personalize and quantify district performance criteria. The **"Look Fors"** and **"Listen Fors"** generated by the staff of Patrick Henry Elementary School, Alexandria City Public Schools, Alexandria, Virginia in a staff meeting facilitated by the Marcia Baldanza, Principal, and the Teacher Leader Cadre are shown on pages 35-36. The teacher leaders and principal do small group walk-throughs on a regular basis and leave an "I Noticed That..." notes as they leave the room. Teachers are comfortable with the process because they became active members of the process when they created the lists of **"Look Fors" and "Listen Fors."**

Walk-Throughs

Remembering What You Saw and Why it was Worth Noticing

Carry a clipboard, note cards, NCR paper...whatever works for you. Take a couple of minutes right after you leave the classroom to jot down key observations and to frame some possible questions about those observations. While forms may be used, care must be taken to ensure that they do not serve as checklists. See **Tools Section** of **Leading the Learning** for examples that have worked well for others.

Feedback

Feedback can be either verbal or written. The format and tone of the feedback is determined by the purpose of the walk-throughs and the context in which the walk-through and the feedback occurs. See the sections of **Leading the Learning** on **Data Collection, Analysis, and Feedback** for detailed information on the options for what to report and how to report it. Given that the decisions we make about the format and tone of the feedback can determine the impact of the feedback on teacher practice and student learning, it is essential that we be thoughtful and informed communicators in any feedback situations. The **ASK Construct** explained on pages 68-69 provides guidance for determining the approach to take.

Feedback Via Conversations and Conferences

In most instances you need no more than 5-10 minutes with each person you observed in a round of walk-throughs. Go to the teacher rather than having the teacher come to you. It may be that if you write a note, you do not have a conversation. If you see something you have seen before and have already "discussed" you may decide that there is no need for a note or a conversation. Be sure that the teacher understands and agrees. If you notice something that is problematic, consider it in context and schedule even more frequent and longer visits to the classroom. Avoid rushing to judgment. If frequent classroom visits to include talking with students and looking at student work are a new process in the building, be careful to ensure that the process becomes established as a positive and productive one rather than being seen as "drive-bys" during which teachers believe observers are trying to catch people being wrong.

The "rules" for walk-throughs should be governed by the purposes of the walk-throughs and the culture/context in which they are done.

Walk-Throughs

Feedback Via Written Notes

Do not create a new paperwork nightmare! Use NCR paper, index cards, or stick-on notes to send quick messages. These formats signal that this process is informal and can become an ongoing part of the school communication system around teaching and learning. Some may choose to send an email. The caution here is to remember the ease with which emails can be forwarded and even changed prior to forwarding.

If the data gathered during walk-throughs is to be part of the body of evidence gathered during an evaluation cycle, be mindful of contractual rulings on the collection, storage, and dissemination of formative and evaluative data.

Carolyn Downey names three types of feedback to use following walk-throughs.
- **Reinforcement:** Noticing and naming teacher or student behavior or classroom environment variables
- **Reflection:** Posing a thought provoking question around rationales, hypothesis, the decision-making process, cause and effect, how data drove decisions, how outcomes matched desired outcomes
- **Refinement:** Suggestions for improvement

It is strongly recommended that while you are in the process of establishing walk-throughs as a positive part of the culture you confine feedback to reinforcement. If cognitive coaching is the norm in your school, then reflective questions should be well received. Refinement suggestions are potentially dangerous to the overall process so consider using the formal observation process for that type of feedback.

Keeping Track

If the purpose of the walk-throughs is to establish a culture in which you, as a principal, coach, or mentor and/or other teachers, routinely do walk-throughs, you will need to develop a system for keeping track of the classes that you visited, when you went, a brief summary of what was observed, and what followed the walk through... a note, conversation, or neither. See the **Tools Section of Leading the Learning** for the form entitled **"Interactions Around Teaching and Learning"** as one possible way to track not only walk-throughs but all interactions around teaching and learning.

Literacy Walk-Through

Focus Question: To what degree is a balanced approach to literacy instruction being implemented?

Teacher(s)_____ Grade Level_____

+ We saw implemented

X We saw evidence that this is used

− We expected to see but did not see

_____Daily read aloud of quality literature
_____Independent reading with self-selected, appropriate books
_____Shared reading: teacher reading while students follow along
_____Small group guided reading
_____Teaching of vocabulary
_____Student responses to reading is meaningful and varied
_____An organized, well-stocked classroom library and reading area
_____Reading opportunities in a variety of genres
_____Teacher modeled writing
_____Shared writing: Teacher writes while composing with students
_____Editing/proofreading expectations students are taught to use resources
     (i.e. word walls, charts) for writing, revising and editing
_____Writing/publishing for real audiences
_____Teaching of conventions: Not through separate exercises, but in process of
     writing
_____Student-selected writing topics
_____Skills instruction is connected to real reading and writing (whole-part-whole)
_____Instruction in "word study" and word-solving strategies
_____Word walls display commonly used words and word patterns, and students
     are held accountable for spelling word wall words correctly
_____Reading/Writing across the curriculum
_____On-going assessment
_____Assessment is used to guide instruction
_____Opportunities for students to share their reading and writing

Other comments: _____

_____

_____

_____

_____

Observers:_____

        _____

        _____

Sharon Edwards and Jacalyn Colt, St. Vrain Valley School District, Longmont, CO

Student Achievement Data

Student Learning is the Goal!

Control and compliance is not the goal! Seat time is not the goal! All students on task is not the goal! It is **student learning** for which we have to hold ourselves accountable. As educational leaders we must build and use, and teach all educators to use, a body of evidence around student learning, including classroom data, data from department, grade level, or district common assessments, as well as state and national assessments.

Analyzing data is not optional and it is not enough. It is the data-driven adjustments we make in our professional practice that make a difference. We must, therefore, get over being defensive about data and use it to inform our practice. **It is the decisions we make and the actions we take as a result of the data analysis for which we need to be held accountable.** What is, is.

As leaders of the learning we need to help teachers build expertise at identifying what data is important, in what situations it is important, and in making sense of it in ways that influence instructional decision making and classroom practice. Whatever data is identified for analysis must be analyzed carefully following the guidelines from best practice in data analysis. Mike Schmoker and Victoria Bernhardt provide us with clear guidelines on how to proceed. Readers should consult their work for in-depth guidance on the process.

Student achievement data should not be the sole data source for teacher evaluation, but it should certainly be included. There is, however, little written about how to do so in a way that does not cause angst. Teachers are quick to become defensive and remind all that will listen that they are not the only teacher these children have ever had and to bring up beyond the school house variables that influence student achievement. Given a lack of exemplars for using student achievement data as part of the supervision and evaluation process we need to create some low risk entry points.

The stages teachers go through to get over being defensive about data to owning the data and the responsibility for responding to that data are varied and **depend greatly on the interactions they have had with colleagues in looking at student work, the relationship they have with their supervisors,** and their very real anxieties about "statistics!" More and more educators are analyzing data but the stumbling block seems to come when action is to follow the analysis. **It is recommended that for now the most productive way, and the way most acceptable to all parties, to include student achievement data in the supervision and evaluation process is to focus on the use of available data to inform instruction.**

Student Achievement Data

Data Analysis for Instructional Decision Making

- Identify and analyze general **trends or patterns** observed. These patterns might be:
  - Identify percentage or number of advanced proficient, proficient, and not proficient
  - Disaggregate data by **demographics** such as gender, ethnicity, time in district, English language proficiency, students on IEPs, and free and reduced lunch (required by No Child Left Behind Act of 2001)
  - Compare current data to **data from past assessments** at this grade level
  - Complete a **longitudinal** comparison of the work of individuals or groups of students over time
- **Analyze data by subsets** such as specific standards, benchmarks, or indicators
- **Cause and effect analysis**
  - Analyze how and when the assessed concepts, facts, and processes were taught
  - Consider which strategies were used
  - Consider what materials were used
  - Consider how much time was allocated
  - Consider the level of thinking the students/student groups now use and the level required by the assessment
  - Review the alignment of the learning experiences with the knowledge, skills, and level of thinking required by the assessment task
  - Ask what changes need to be made the next time these points are taught or to whom they should be retaught
- **Compare classroom assessment data and external assessment data**
- **Do an item analysis**
  - Which items were missed by most students
  - Which items were missed by highest performing students
  - Which items were missed by almost proficient students
  - Which items were missed by special needs students
  - Which items were missed by second language learners
- **Create tables that show the data by students, by subgroup, my item, or broader categories such as benchmarks or standards**

Following the data analysis, identify the baseline data for which targets will be set. Identify targets and then make action plans based on what was learned from the data analysis.

See Tool-23: Item Analysis. See Tool-24: Cause/Effect Analysis. See Tool-27: Student Impact Plan.

Cause/Effect Analysis

Cause/Effect Analysis and Revision Planner for Family Unit

Standard: History 6 - Students know that religious and philosophical ideas have been powerful forces throughout history.

Benchmark: 6.1 Know the historical development of religions and philosophies:

Indicator: The student can recognize and describe family customs, traditions, and beliefs.

Desired Effect - What were the **desired** group and/or individual assessment results? Given 100% **Not Proficient** on narrative pre-assessment. At Least 75% of students scoring **Proficient**, or **Above Proficient** and no score **Not Proficient** on overall

Effect - What were the **actual** group and/or individual assessment results? 88% **Proficient** or **Above Proficient** and 0% **Not Proficient** BUT on narrative post-assessment 28% **Proficient** or **Above Proficient** and 33% **Not Proficient** (structure and technology made a difference)

Cause: Methods

Methods used this time:
- Literature
- Class discussions
- Guest speaker
- Individual family inquiry
- Modeling/scaffolding

Potential changes for next time:
- Concentrate on origin & describing practice
- More modeling
- More peer sharing

Cause: People

People involved this time:
- Teacher
- Peer
- Family

Potential changes for next time:
- Have students interview family about specific family customs, traditions, or beliefs including origins
- Oral sharing with peers before post

Cause: Materials

Materials used this time:
- Paper and pencil
- Computer with KidPix program

Potential changes for next time:
- Better organizer for outlining presentation
- More fine tuned naming & saving process
- Organization matrix to report responses on pre- and post-assessments

Cause: Time

Time used this time:
- 5 days planning
- 9 days designing
- One session

Potential changes for next time:
- Use timeline for how long to work on each page to help with time management
- Possibly more than one session

Planning and Reflective Journals

Journals are both a data collection tool and a professional growth tool. This makes them an excellent means of communication for many professionals. They are, in fact, a non-threatening self-assessment tool. They play an important role in moving a portfolio to portfolio status rather than the collection of artifacts that simply are a scrapbook that is a grown-up "show and tell." They help answer the "**so what**" and "**what if**" questions about the events of our professional work.

Journals are an excellent way to gather data about the work teachers do beyond the classroom. This is true whether the work is in preparation for or a reflection about classroom work or a record of planning, decision making, actions, and reflections about work with other teachers, as well as project design and implementation.

Teachers on Special Assignment or in Leadership Roles

Brenda Kaylor, Director of Professional Development in St. Vrain Valley School District, Longmont, Colorado, has the induction coaches and clinical professors she supervises keep journals throughout their three years in those positions. She reads them at least once a quarter and responds in writing. This sort of review and response allows a supervisor to offer support or to reframe the thinking of the journal writer in gentle but direct ways.

A review of the coaches' journals reveals incredible professional growth over time. An interesting component of those journals is the use of the **ASK Construct** which structures the annual goals the coaches and clinicals set for themselves. They place these **ASK Goals** in the front of their journals and this provides the frame for reading the journal and analyzing the learning journey. See page 68-69 for an explanation of the **ASK Construct** and **Tool-25** to use in formatting goals.

Dialogue Journals

A dialogue journal can be kept in a traditional journal format, be a printout of computer entries or kept electronically. The critical attribute is the text dialogue between the teacher and the supervisor, mentor, or coach. When geography or time constraints limit the frequency of face-to-face interactions these journals can be a productive way to fill the gaps. They can only be effective if response turnaround time is quick, if the two parties trust one another, and this form of communication matches the information processing styles of both parties.

Planning and Reflective Journals

Journal Organization

Journals can be organized chronologically or thematically. Teachers might decide to keep their journal entries sorted by areas of performance used by the districts supervision and evaluation system. This is a good approach if the journals are to become part of a portfolio.

Possible entries or sections include:
- goals and action plans
- success or problems with a lesson, unit, program, training session, work session, etc.
- parent-teacher conferences
- professional development experiences
- interactions with peers
  - collaborating
  - coaching
  - mentoring
  - problem identifying and solving
  - dealing with different perspectives
- interactions with individual students or the entire class
- daily thinking...aha's and questions, general musings
- responses to discussions, professional development opportunities or professional readings
- set priorities and schedules
- identify and solve problems
- record and evaluate practices and effectiveness of efforts

Self-Assessment

According to Airasian and Gullickson (1997), teacher self-assessment is an important process because, among other reasons, it:
- is a professional responsibility
- focuses professional development and improvement on the classroom or school level where teachers have their greatest expertise and effect
- recognizes that organizational change is usually the result of individuals changing themselves and their personal practices, not of "top-down" mandates
- makes teachers aware of the strengths and weaknesses of their practice, which grows from the immediacy and complexity of the classroom as do teachers' motives and incentives
- encourages ongoing teacher development and discourages unchanging classroom beliefs, routines, and methods

Any use of self-assessment as part of the supervision and evaluation process is **best done voluntarily on the part of the teacher** and is included in the process as only **one of several components.** The use of other terms such as action research, examining student work, journaling, reflective logs and discussions, etc., may be less threatening than the use of the term self-assessment. In fact, each of the approaches listed in the previous sentence are methods of self assessment.

Self-assessment can take the form of questionnaires and checklists, videotaped teaching episodes with critique, portfolio preparation, analysis of student work, and many other formats.

Teachers can complete a self assessment either before writing a professional development plan, during the year or the evaluation cycle as a benchmarking tool, or as part of a summative reflection on their professional growth and the impact of their efforts on student learning and school improvement.

Possible questions to help teachers reflect on the year and to consider in developing a professional development plan include:
- What has been the most positive aspect of your instructional practice over the past few years?
- What area of instruction gives you the most difficulty?
- If you had last year to do over, what would you change?
- What are some of your activities or ideas that you would share with others?
- What would you like to learn more about, whether it be from another teacher, a special training program, or other resources?
- In working with parents/guardians, what skills do you possess that allow for positive and productive outcomes?
- What are your strengths as a teacher?
- What areas of your teaching would you like to improve?

Self-Assessment

Another format might be to construct a **survey** in which a teacher indicates their attitudes, skills, and knowledge about topics considered important in instructional decision making.

Topics might include:
- Inclusion
- Performance assessment
- Multiple intelligences theory
- Constructivism
- Critical thinking skills
- Metacognition
- Differentiation
- Literacy
- Examining student work

Variables could include:
- familiar, heard the term, unfamiliar
- very important, somewhat important, not important at this time
- integrated into practice, learning about it, not yet a focus

The supervisor, coach and/or teacher could use the results to identify areas for professional growth and further identify needed support systems and time frames for study and reporting back on progress.

See **Tool 28: Year End Reflections** and see page 61 for excerpts from Monson, Massachusetts, Professional Practice Profile Self-Assessment.

Professional Practice Profile Self-Assessment

Directions: The Massachusetts Professional Practice Profile is divided into five areas.

- **Plans Curriculum and Instruction**
- **Delivers Effective Instruction**
- **Creates a Positive and Productive Environment**
- **Promotes Equity and an Appreciation of Diversity**
- **Meets Professional Responsibilities**

Each area is broken down into standards and each standard has descriptors/indicators and examples of evidence. Read the listed standards and mark where you think you are on the continuum for each standard - **Not Yet, Work in Progress,** or **In Place and Functioning Smoothly.** You may choose to color code or date your marks on the continuum so you can see changes over time. Use the **Reflection** at the end of each section to summarize where you think you are.

Plans Curriculum and Instruction

1. Draws on content of the relevant curriculum framework to plan activities addressing standards that will advance students' level of content knowledge and skills.

Not Yet	Work in Progress	In Place and Functioning Smoothly

2. Plans sequential units of study that make learning cumulative, connect learning across disciplines, and are based on the learning standards within the frameworks.

Not Yet	Work in Progress	In Place and Functioning Smoothly

3. Draws on results of formal and informal assessments and knowledge of human development to plan learning activities appropriate for the range of students within a classroom.

Not Yet	Work in Progress	In Place and Functioning Smoothly

4. Integrates technology and media in the management of the work of teaching and in student learning.

| Not Yet | Work in Progress | In Place and Functioning Smoothly |

5. Uses information in Individual Education Plans (IEPs), 504 Plans, and District Curriculum Accommodation Plans (DCAP) to plan strategies for integrating students with special needs into regular classrooms.

| Not Yet | Work in Progress | In Place and Functioning Smoothly |

Reflections: What are my strengths in planning curriculum and instruction? Which characteristics need strengthening or improvement? What is the data

Promotes Equity and an Appreciation of Diversity

1. Acts on the belief that all students can master a challenging curriculum and includes all students in the range of academic opportunities and in higher order thinking.

| Not Yet | Work in Progress | In Place and Functioning Smoothly |

2. Assesses the significance of student differences in performance levels, learning styles, cultural heritage, language, socio-economic backgrounds, and physical and emotional disabilities and adapts classroom activities appropriately.

| Not Yet | Work in Progress | In Place and Functioning Smoothly |

Reflections: What are my strengths in promoting equity and an appreciation of diversity? What standards need strengthening or improvement? What is the data?

Louise Thompson, ASK Group Consultant, in collaboration with the Monson, MA Supervision and Evaluation Process Revision Committee
Standards/Indicators from *Teaching Matters*, a MASSPARTNERS Position Paper

Looking at Teacher Work

The Planning Process

A review of lesson plan books reveals that, in many cases, teachers write topics and/or page numbers as their "lesson plans." While these words and numbers may well be code for much more complex thinking and planning, teachers need to be able to communicate that thinking in either written or oral form. Supervisors, mentors, and coaches need to guide teachers to consider not only what they are teaching, but why they are teaching it, how they are teaching it, and when they are teaching it.

One of the biggest challenges facing teachers in a standards-based environment is the **planning process**. It can be an even bigger challenge for supervisors because many do not have experience with this process. While many districts have had curriculum guides for years, for some teachers how closely those guides were followed was a matter of personal choice. In fact, in many districts staff proudly pointed out the autonomy with which teachers engaged in their practice. In a standards-based environment there is still a great deal of autonomy around how to instruct, but much more external direction and accountability about what to teach and how the learning will be measured. **This external direction and accountability demands that the planning process function like a well oiled machine and that means that supervisors, mentors, and coaches must include discussions about it their supervisory interactions.**

Planning and pacing for the year needs to precede unit design to ensure that time is appropriately allocated throughout the year for the essential knowledge and skills. In past practice we often started at the beginning of the book and worked our way through the chapters and, of course, ran out of time before we reached the end of the book. One often hears the phrase " I have so much to cover" in reference to this march through the pages. If the school district has not mapped the curriculum or developed pacing guides, discussions need to be held with teachers around their thinking about how they map out the year. It is only after that thinking is done that units of study can be designed with some assurance that there is sufficient time in the instructional calendar to devote to each unit. The **Operator's Guide to the Standard's Based Classroom,** listed in Instructional Resources and References, provides printable forms for the planning process from planning for the year to examining the cause and effect of teacher decision making of students achievement

See pages 164-165 for key points to consider when reviewing lesson and unit plans. The **Tools** section includes several forms to use in guiding the instructional planning process. These **Tools** are listed on page 166.

Points to Note in the
Review of a Standards-Based Unit

Hundreds of teachers each year use the components listed below to design standards-based units during ASK Group workshops. They design units, write out all the components, teach the unit, and in an informal peer review process, present their plan, student work, and planned revisions to colleagues.

While it may not be necessary for teachers to write out all the components for each unit they teach, it is necessary that they develop and practice using a framework that guides their thinking about planning units in a standards-based environment. Supervisors, mentors, and coaches need to review the unit planning process with staff so that they can become informed about this type of unit and can then, in turn, support staff in learning to use the process well and consistently.

- Addresses district **standards, benchmarks, and indicators**

- Includes an assessment or **set of assessments** that allow students to demonstrate what they know and what they can do with what they know

- Incorporates **preassessment, formative and summative assessment** components

- Uses assessment strategies that allow students to demonstrate what they know in different ways

- Provides **public and precise criteria** for success that is to be communicated to learners prior to beginning the work; if possible, exemplars are also provided

- Includes a thorough and detailed **task analysis** of the standards, benchmarks, and/or indicators and of the assessment task

- Includes **instructional strategies that address the knowledge and skills identified by the task analysis**

- Includes instructional strategies that **frame the learning** and learning experiences that help students **make connections** and process their learning in ways that promote retention and transfer to new situations

- Provides **accommodations and differentiation** for a wide range of learners

- Includes plans for revision based on **data and analysis of student work**

- Reveals evidence of **collegial collaboration** in planning, implementing, and/or revising the unit

See pages 31-54 in *Instruction for All Students* and pages 169-192 in *Why Didn't I Learn This in College?* for detailed information on the SBE Planning Process.

Lesson Plan Review

Being skilled at writing clear and focused lesson plans does not guarantee that the teacher can implement the plan in a way that engages all students in meaningful learning. Without such a plan, however, the likelihood of the design and delivery of lessons that are rigorous, coherent, engaging, and aligned to the district standards is greatly decreased. It is much better to have a plan to adjust than it is to rely on textbook publishers or the designers of curriculum programs. No matter how thorough the support provided by text and curriculum manuals, it is the teacher actions in the classroom that determine whether or not students will learn at high levels.

As an Ongoing Process Throughout The Year

In some school districts teachers are asked to submit lesson plans for the upcoming week. Often the process includes only an accountability checking to see if the plans were submitted rather than an examination of rigor, coherency, potential for engagement, and the alignment with district standards. This implementation of "lesson plan review" is no more productive than simply checking to see if the students did their homework or not. In both cases we need to be asking whether or not the work is the right work.

During the evaluation cycle, lesson plans should reflect a use of the learning and suggestions that have occurred during other interactions and/or been presented in observation reports or other informal feedback.

In some school districts teachers are asked to have their lesson plans out and available in their classrooms for observers whenever they come into the classroom. A quick scan of the lesson plans is a valuable tool for supervisors, mentors, and coaches because it provides immediate context for what is being observed. Knowing what the intent of the learning exercises is helps frame the questions you ask the students, the way you listen to teacher comments, and the way you analyze the learning environment.

As a Component of the Planning Conference

To promote reflective practice and to make the planning conference a professional development opportunity teachers might be asked to complete written reflections on their instructional plans for the instructional period during which a formal observation will be conducted and then submit the reflection prior to the conference. When the questions asked are reflective rather than a listing of what is to occur, the discussion during the conference can be far more productive for the teacher and for the principal who gains insight into the decision making process the teacher is using.

Instructional Planning Tools

SBE Planning Process: Tool-32

This tool can be used to explain the SBE planning process in its simplest way. Text to support the tool can be found in *Why Didn't I Learn This in College?* on page 175.

Unit Review: Tool-33

This one page tool is designed to be a quick analysis of the presence of the essential components of a standards-based unit with boxes in which to jot down the data.

Unit Plan A: Tool-34

This one page tool is one to be used as starting point in the design of a standards-based unit. It might be used to capture ideas for specific units as teachers are mapping out the year.

Unit Plan B: Tool-35

This two page unit planner is a favorite of new teachers. It addresses the essential components of a standards-based unit and includes a place to determine the sequence and time allocations for the unit.

Lesson Planning Guide: Tool-36

This one page lesson planning guide is useful as a tool for communicating lesson plans to supervisors, mentors, or coaches prior to planning conferences and for capturing the key ideas about daily lessons.

Task Analysis: Tool-37

This tool provides T-Charts on which teachers can identify the knowledge and skills required by summative assessment tasks. Support materials for this tool can be found in *Instruction for All Students* on pages 46-47 and *Why Didn't I Learn This in College?* on page 185.

Top Ten Questions I Ask Myself: Tool-38

This multiple page tool provides spaces for recording answers to the planning questions addressed in *Instruction for All Students*. Page references to locate the guidelines for answers are included.

Looking at Teacher Work

Instructional Materials

All professionals throughout their careers collect resources to enhance their knowledge and skills. It is foolish to think that teachers can teach using one set of textbooks and a teachers manual. Given that, it makes sense that we include in the supervisory and evaluation process inquiries about what resources teachers are using and how they go about finding new content material and instructional strategies. On a walk through the social studies department at New Trier High School, Winnetka, Illinois, one sees an extensive personal collection of books related to history and the social sciences at each teacher's work station. These are not classroom materials but rather a wide array of background materials for the teacher. While a bookshelf full of books is not worthy of note on its own merit, questions about why these books and how they are used can provide valuable insight into the instructional planning processes in which the teacher engages.

All classrooms are enhanced by multiple sources of information for students. Some of these are provided by the school system and some are acquired over time by individual teachers. When visiting classrooms, make note of the materials that have been gathered and displayed for student use. Include discussions about the rationale for those particular books, charts, manipulatives and how they are used to strengthen the instructional program.

Classroom Assessments to Include Criteria & Exemplars

Few educators have had extensive training around the selection or design of traditional assessments. In recent years many have participated in at least minimal professional development around performance assessment. Supervisors, mentors, and coaches may well find that they are lacking the knowledge and skills to assess the appropriateness of either traditional or performance assessments, or the criteria used to assess student work. This lack of knowledge and skills may lead to an avoidance of asking hard questions about whether or not these classroom assessments provide rehearsals for high stakes assessments and about whether or not a thorough task analysis has been completed in order to design learning experiences that prepare students for success on the assessments. Ask teachers to bring assessments, rubrics, performance task lists, or checklists and exemplars of student work that meets and does not meet standards. A supervisory or coaching conference around what can be done to help those who have not met standards would be a good use of time.

Looking at Teacher Work

Action Research

See the **Contexts** section of this book for information on action research. It is addressed as a potential data source in supervision and evaluation of competent teachers in **Tool-27: Student Impact Plan**.

Records Review

This data source is particularly valuable in working with special educators and counselors, but is also important for classroom teachers. Records to be considered when working with classroom teachers are plan books, grade books, attendance records, school policy manuals, learning standards, information on special needs of students, and appropriate records of interactions with students, colleagues, and parents. For special educators, managing the amount of paper work required is astonishing and worthy of note by supervisors and possibly indicate a need for coaching or mentoring expertise. Counselors, of course, have the responsibility of tracking course completion, graduation requirements, and ongoing,, although possibly irregular, contacts with students, teachers, and parents. For all educators, a discussion about organizational systems and compliance with school, district, state, and national regulations is one that should not be left until there is a problem.

Parent Communications

Almost all professional performance evaluation criteria include one or more indicators around parent communications. This, too, is not a variable to leave until there is a problem. Clearly articulated school philosophy, expectations, and procedures on working with parents should be followed by supervisory, coaching, and mentoring conversations about the effectiveness and the efficiency of those communications. For suggestions to offer teachers in working with parents see Chapter X in *Why Didn't I Learn This in College?* titled "Parents as Partners." This chapter provides many tips for working with parents in a positive and collaborative way.

Portfolios

Portfolios provide a wonderful opportunity for teachers to demonstrate both the depth and breadth of their expertise and their commitment to analysis and reflection. Portfolios are the basis of certification by the National Board for Professional Teaching Standards (NTPTS). See www.nbpts.org for lengthy and detailed directions and exemplars of their requirements in each discipline.

Preparing even a "regular," non-NTPTS, portfolio can be a daunting task for busy classroom teachers. Interestingly enough it is not the collection of artifacts that seems daunting; it is the reflection on the significance of the artifacts. When using portfolios as a method of data collection, it is essential that there be interim checkpoints along the way so teachers do not end up at the due date staying up all night putting the finishing reflective touches on the portfolios. For those who are naturally reflective and inclined to keep a journal or log, a portfolio is an excellent choice. For those who are not so inclined, it may be a painful experience. Given what we know about the power of face-to-face interaction and dialogue it might be possible to have teachers put together their portfolios and then do an oral presentation about the contents. Another possibility to consider is a team portfolio.

For purposes of supervision and evaluation it makes sense to organize portfolios around the Areas of Professional Performance. The use of an artifact checklist or index card file to track what is being collected can help identify gaps and help teachers begin to think more purposefully about what data needs to be gathered to fully represent the work in each area. See the next page for Artifact Possibilities.

A **working portfolio** is one in which you place all the artifacts you find that would represent your teaching. Setting up a crate with a hanging file folder for each Area of Performance is one way to begin collecting and sorting artifacts. Later you can select the prime artifacts to include in a presentation portfolio. More is not necessarily better! The final **presentation portfolio** should include a rationale for each piece in the portfolio explicitly tying it to one of the teaching standards, an analysis of its usefulness and a reflection on what you learned from the event. While the NBPTS portfolios include only samples of students' work, videotapes of classroom practice, and documentation of accomplishments outside the classroom, there are many possible artifacts to consider. The following list provides some possibilities.

Artifact Possibilities

Raso Stone, elementary art teacher, in St. Vrain Valley School District, Longmont, Colorado keeps her portfolio up-to-date and available to parents to peruse when they come in for conferences.

- Anecdotal records
- Audiotapes of student work
- Awards and certificates
- Bulletin board displays of student work (photos)
- Class newspapers
- Classroom assessments
- Collaborative efforts
- Computer use for organization
- Computer use for instruction
- Course syllabus
- Extracurricular/co-curricular documentation
- Grant proposals/grants received
- Lesson and unit plans
- Letters of recommendation
- Individualized plans
- Interest inventories
- Interviews with students, teachers and parents

- Journals
- Letters to parents
- Letters from parents
- Letters of recommendation
- Observation reports
- Organizational strategies
- Performance evaluations
- Philosophy statement
- Pictures and photographs
- Problem-solving logs
- Professional development plans
- Professional development organized and led
- Professional organizations
- Professional readings list
- Publications
- Resume
- Rubrics and performance assessment task lists
- Self-assessments
- Student achievement goals, action plans, and results
- Student work
- Teacher-made instructional materials
- Use of professional learning documentation
- Videotapes

Shadowing

This data source is especially useful with professionals who do not have full-time direct classroom responsibility for teaching K-12 students. Shadowing is similar to an **Informal Observation** but different in that these staff members may be working one-on-one with a student or a parent and may be operating in an office setting rather than in a classroom. Such staff members include counselors, psychologists, itinerant teachers, case managers, and therapists. Issues of confidentiality should not stand in the way of shadowing, but utmost care must be taken to respect the confidentiality inherent in the work of these staff members.

The analysis of data gathered would be based on the job description of the staff member and appropriate indicators from the district's criteria for professional performance. A **Planning Conference** or a **Structured Interview** conducted in advance of a **Shadowing** would be invaluable in providing context for what is observed.

Many of the indicators included in the district's criteria for professional performance should apply to people in this positions. The selection of other indicators would be determined by the job description of the staff member. Using the district's four to six broad standards or domains indicators can easily be developed to match job descriptions. In some instances the term **"interaction"** may reasonably replace the term **"instruction"**.

Structured Interview

This data source is useful with all staff but is especially useful with those who do not have full-time direct responsibility for teaching K-12 students. Given a goal of better understanding the decision making process being used by staff this data source is useful in capturing the planning, designing, reflecting, adjusting, and growth of all staff members. Should you be in the position of having not taught the grade level or course taught by the teacher or having not held the position held by the staff member, a structured interview around the job description and a collaborative analysis of the district's performance criteria could lead to the creation of a useful set of indicators.

Any indicators included in the district's criteria for professional performance can be translated into structured interview questions. The selection of indicators is determined by the job description of the staff member. Additional questions would come from the district job description, or if it is a "customized" position to meet particular school needs, then the questions would come from the job description created for that position.

See the following page for an example of a structured interview as part of hiring process.

Beginning with the End in Mind: A fully qualified and fully satisfied teacher in every classroom. The hiring interview is our first opportunity to gather data about teacher attitudes, skills, and knowledge. Design the interview questions around the district performance criteria and district and school priorities.

Patrick Henry Elementary School
Interview Questions for Teacher Applicants

Thank you for your interest in teaching and learning at Patrick Henry Elementary School. Below are six important areas for success in any grade level or in any role at our school (Rutherford, 2002). Questions are asked from each area to help us determine your content knowledge and your collaborative fit. Review them and we'll be with you shortly.

Planning Instruction
- How do you translate "beginning with the end in mind" into planning and pacing for the year, the unit, and the lesson?

Implementing Instruction
- How do you frame the learning for students?
- When and why do you ask questions of students?
- Give examples of active learning strategies in your repertoire

Assessing Learning and the Instructional Program
- How do you make sure students are ready to learn?
- How are you sure they are on the learning journey with you?
- How are you sure they caught what you taught?

Orchestrating a Positive Learning Environment
- Define praise, encouragement, and feedback. How do you use them in a positive learning environment?
- What four qualities exist in a good place to learn?
- How do you deal with unmet expectations?

Leading a Productive Learning-Centered Environment
- What is a learning-centered classroom and what do you do to create and lead in such a learning environment?
- How do you get and keep students' attention?
- Discuss classroom interior design
- How do you group students?

Professional and Collegial Collaboration
- How do you build positive and productive relationships with parents?
- What does collaboration mean to you?
- Not all groups are teams: How will you know you're on a team, and not just part of a group? What will you contribute to our teams?

See Tool-30: Interview Questions for Teacher Positions

Documentation for those in
Beyond the Classroom Roles

Teacher Leadership Roles

Teachers assume many professional responsibilities beyond the classroom. We need to be purposeful in documenting and providing feedback on their performance in those roles. In some cases teachers assume these responsibilities in addition to their classroom responsibilities and sometimes they work full-time in the leadership roles. The following list is representative of the positions teachers hold that may require a variety of data sources beyond what we use in documenting the performance of the classroom teacher.

- **Teacher on Special Assignment**
- **Mentor**
- **Coach (Induction, Literacy, Math, etc.)**
- **Department Chair**
- **Team Leader**
- **Curriculum Design**
- **Professional Development Facilitator**
- **Instructional Advisory Board**
- **Program Coordinator**
- **Reading Specialist**

It is essential that certain elements be clearly articulated before we can supervise and evaluate teachers in these roles. The elements include:

- **Clear criteria**
- **Program goals**
- **System financial and political realities**

Data sources include:

- **Goals accompanied by action plans**
- **Informal observations**
- **Program and session evaluations**
- **Journals**
- **Shadowing**
- **Structured interviews**
- **Student achievement data**
- **Student work (adults and children)**

See an example of structured interview questions that could be used with

Documentation for those in
Beyond the Classroom Roles

secondary department chairs on pages 175-176. Design a series of questions or queries that match the job description of the teachers serving in the role of department chair. Use the questions with all department chairs to gather both teacher evaluation data and program evaluation data. Lynn Nice used similar questions as part of the Fairfax County Public Schools, Fairfax, Virginia, Principal Performance Evaluation Program conversations with department chairs and team leaders. Providing staff members with the questions in advance provides clarity about expectations and focus for the work.

Library Media Specialists, Counselors, Psychologists, Therapists, and Social Workers

All the world is a classroom! A review of professional performance criteria documents from many school districts reveals that the same broad standards areas or domains are appropriate for, and are used for, specialists working with students in settings other than the traditional classroom setting. While there is some slight language change in the indicators and some additional indicators determined by job descriptions in a given district, all are focused on student learning and creating conditions to promote that learning.

Secondary Department Chair
Structured Interview

- Describe your role in the **hiring/mentoring process** for new teachers. What systems are in place in the department to assist new or struggling teachers?

- Describe **programs or pilots** that are being implemented in the department in support of district and school initiatives.

- Describe efforts to increase and ensure opportunities for **professional growth** in the areas targeted in school and departmental goals.

- How does the department actively solicit **parental support**, inform the parents of departmental offerings, the standards of learning for the courses, and the connections between the courses?

- How are department members engaged in **collaborative decision making** around issues like the master schedule, course offerings, number of preparations, and room assignments?

- Explain the processes that are in place to ensure that instruction is focused on the **learning standards** identified by the district.

- Describe the ways the department is working to create **common assessments** aligned with standards.

- Explain how **student achievement data** is used to inform both departmental decision and classroom instruction.

- Describe **grading issues** that have surfaced and how those have been resolved. Include issues such as variances in grading policies, grade distributions, disputed grades.

- Share some examples across several teachers that would provide evidence of **learning-centered instruction**.

- Describe how the department addresses issues of **minority and gender enrollments** in upper level, International Baccalaureate, and Advanced Placement courses. What actions have been taken and what are the results?

- What are you doing about **courses that cause concern** because of high D/F rates, low or decreasing enrollments, dropout rates, skewed enrollment by gender or ethnicity?

- Describe how the department is **integrating technology** into instruction.

- How are you resolving any equipment shortages or resistance to using **technology as a learning tool**?

Secondary Department Chair
Structured Interview

- Describe the **communication systems** used within the department, with others in the school, and with the district.

- Describe the objectives, agendas, and frequency of **department meetings**. How are they designed and what are the systems for following up on discussion or decision items?

Leading the Learning

Providing Growth Producing Feedback

Feedback

The Change Process and Adult Learners
Communication Skills
Consulting, Collaborating, and Coaching
Difficult Conferences
Observation Reports
Evaluation Reports
Improvement Plans

This section focuses on how we use what we have observed, read, and heard to guide those we are charged with leading to be thoughtful and data-driven in their own decision making and professional practice. The data is gathered and analyzed, now what? The essential questions addressed are:

- What knowledge, skills, and attitudes do I need to master in order to engage competent teachers in conversations and conferences that lead to teacher growth, decision making, and action in the interest of student learning?

- How do I work with teachers who are ineffective or not receptive to suggestions and directions?

Feedback: How Learning Occurs

> "Feedback is information about how we did in light of what we attempted. Intent vs. effect. Actual vs. ideal performance. The best feedback is highly specific, descriptive of what we did and did not do in light of standards, and occurs in both a timely and ongoing way. Think of the best feedback systems: computer games, your shower faucets, or tasting the meal as you cook. Or recall how often the music or tennis coach provides a steady flow of feedback to show you how your actions cause this or that result.... What feedback most certainly isn't is praise and blame or mere encouragement."
>
> **Grant Wiggins**

"Feedback is information about how we did in light of what we attempted." If we can agree that **"what we are attempting"** is always increased student learning, then we know how to focus the feedback we give and the questions we ask. That focus alone would change the way we supervise and mentor teachers. A first step in improving our supervisory practice then is to begin by asking, **"How did this lesson help students learn?"** rather than "How do you think it went?" While the latter may have the same intent, it is not as explicit.

We want the teachers with whom we work, as well as ourselves, to be able to self-assess, to know when to ask for coaching, and then to be able to self-adjust in order to promote student learning.. That, of course, is not the case for many of us. Given that, supervisors, mentors, and coaches need great knowledge and skill around how adults receive and respond to data, feedback, and new ideas. While some of us do this work quite well intuitively, as Madeline Hunter said, "Intuition is no substitute for competence!"

As leaders of adult learning, we never know when a teachable moment will occur. Both carefully planned conferences and informal hallway conversations can have a powerful influence on teacher decision making and classroom practice. To that end, we need to be purposeful about building skills for engaging in those conversations and conferences.

Seven variables to consider in both informal conversations and conferences are:
- **The Change Process**
- **How Adults Learn**
- **Information Processing**
- **Communication Skills**
- **Stages of Development**
- **Attitudes, Skills, and Knowledge of the Teacher**
- **Data Driven Discussions**

Change Happens!

The Realities of the Change Process

- Change happens... it either happens to you or you make it happen!
- Some experts say that we fear change. Others say that we can deal just fine with change; we just cannot give up what we already know and do, so we try to do it all.
- Change takes place in a context. Too much change at once can cause, at least momentarily, chaos or paralysis.
- Organizations do not change; individuals change.
- Changes takes place at different speeds depending on how much else is changing and how different the change is from current practice or knowledge.
- Change takes time.
- Change is hard to sustain.
- Some people seek or cause change; others avoid it.
- Many say cynically of changes in the context of new initiatives, "This too shall pass," so they just wait it out.

What Does Change Look Like in Schools?

Given tenure and the seemingly unending need for more teachers in most fields, there is job security in public education beyond that found in other arenas. Yet, when change in the form of **new approaches, new programs, new standards, new administrators, and certainly, new accountability measures** is introduced, there is often a sense of anxiety and even resistance. This may be caused by our tendency to have an endless series of new initiatives annually instead of engaging in long-term sustained and integrated initiatives. It may be caused by the fact that people who enter the field of public education often are more comfortable maintaining the status quo than in charting new courses. Another variable may be that changes are often announced without any effort to explain the rationale or assess the readiness levels of the people who have to implement the change. The possibilities for one-on-one professional development through the supervision and evaluation process should not be missed.

Leadership for Change

A focus on learners and learning should be the lens through which all change is considered, initiated, and supported. When new ideas are put forth always ask, **"How will this help students learn?"** If we frame change in the interest of student learning, it is more difficult for anyone to resist.

Growth-Producing Feedback

Because adults...

- need to be validated for what they already know and do, **we need to recognize and build on their experience**

- experience a dip in their sense of self-efficacy when new initiatives with new skills and language are introduced, **we need to provide encouragement and recognition of effort**

- as K-12 teachers spend much of their time with children, **they need opportunities to be congenial and socialize at the beginning of conferences and work sessions**

- should be offered choice in how they learn, as long as what they are learning is based on the mission and vision of the organization and is in the interest of student learning, **we need to provide multiple learning formats and environments**

- internalize and use strategies that they experience far better than they internalize strategies that they only hear or read about, **we need to structure our interactions to include opportunities for staff to experience proven teaching/learning strategies**

- engage when they are asked what they would like to know about the topic, **we need a repertoire of ways to gather, analyze, and use the data about their concerns, goals, and needs**

- need to see and hear examples from situations similar to the ones in which they work, **we need to locate and save examples from all content areas and grade levels**

- want to know why and how the supervisor, mentor, or coach is qualified to lead their learning and whether or not the leader has "walked the talk," **we need to be storytellers...but not braggarts**

- respond to humor, **we need to be able to enjoy the moment and, as appropriate, build in humorous stories**

- expect feedback on work they do, **we need to not only give them appropriate feedback, we need to teach them strategies and protocols for asking for and giving each other feedback**

Information Processing

Our own personal experiences combined with our natural tendencies to process information in certain ways makes influencing or guiding our thinking a complex endeavor. We should never underestimate the power of understanding how others view the world and the lens through which they process events, information, and authority. If we can predict or at least consider why people react and respond the way they do to us, to new initiatives, to new directions, to conflicting information, to financial and political realities, and to data, we can better frame our presentations, responses, and interventions.

On the surface, **no way is better than any other way**. The leadership dilemma is the need to step out of our own comfort zones in order to establish cognitive empathy, to think like the other person is thinking. Use the list below to assess your own tendencies and then read through it again trying to see the world the way you think the person with whom you are conversing or conferencing does. Once you identify the potential differences, you can plan how to accommodate them.

Do You Hear What I Say? Do I Hear What You Say?

introverted or extroverted: Do you prefer to respond to new information immediately doing your thinking out loud or do you prefer information in advance so that you have time to think about the issues before you have to respond?

global or analytical: Do you tend to see the big picture and like to have scaffolding on which to hang details or do you prefer to see the bits and pieces and then put them into the whole?

random or sequential: Do you prefer to work through steps in sequence or are you more inclined to jump around and deal with ones that interest you in the moment?

concrete or abstract: Do you want to see the real thing rather than hear about the theory or the possibilities?

sensing or feeling: Do you prefer to deal with what you can see, hear, and touch or do you prefer to go with gut instincts?

in the moment or in the past or in the future: Is what happened in the past, what is happening right now, or what the future will bring that matters most?

decisive or open ended: Do you tend to make quick decisions and stand by them or do you prefer to continue to gather information and have several options?

head or heart: Do you lead primarily with your head or your heart? Do you say "I think" or "I feel?"

Information Processing

Do You Hear What I Say? Do I Hear What You Say?

why or how: Which question is the first to come to your mind when someone presents information, "Why is that a good idea?" or "How would that look?"

observer or hands-on active learner: Do you learn best by observing from a distance or do you need to get into the action and mess around with new ideas and processes?

research or personal practice experience: Do you tend to seek out and cite research or do you prefer to rely on past experience?

plan ahead or wait until last minute: Do you finish projects well in advance and put them away until needed or are you inclined to fill all available time no matter when you start?

internal attributions or external attributions: Do you tend to question the effectiveness of your own efforts or attribute success or failure to the variables that are beyond your control?

negative or positive: Do you view the world through a rose-colored lens or are you more likely to see problems just around the corner?

logical or intuitive: Do you prefer to measure and quantify things or are you comfortable with knowing without knowing how you know?

systems thinker or focused personal view: Do you think more about how actions and information impact the complex organization around you or do you focus on the world right around you?

position power or personal power: Do you define authority primarily by the titles people hold or from the respect they have earned?

After you have assessed your own view of the world and made your best predictions about the person or persons with whom you are working, it is important that you not think that you have the correct view and they have the wrong one. It is a waste of energy to try to convince them to see the world through your lens. The information or data that you want to share does not change. **The way you present the information or data is the variable that can be adjusted in order to promote acceptance, understanding, and action.**

Stages of Development

Just Tell Me What To Do!

- Know one way and, for the moment, want to know only one way to do something
- Seek the cookbook that provides strategies guaranteed to work all the time
- Make good faith effort to do as told and may feel inadequate if it does not work
- Give up easily and quickly abandon new strategies when they do not work perfectly
- Focus on the classroom and the learners for whom they have direct responsibilities
- Little interest in departmental and school initiatives
- Want a supervisor who is willing to tell them what to do, when it should be done, how to do it, and one who recognizes that they are giving their best effort

Are You Sure? I Think That...

- Begin to ask more questions
- Are hearing about and becoming more interested in different points of view
- May begin to resist direction from authority figures
- Prefer to be engaged in collaborative efforts where options are put forth and they can decide which to try and which to ignore
- Want a supervisor who appreciates that they are finding their own voices, celebrates and encourages that, and can change approaches in mid-sentence

Let's Talk!

- Want to be active participants in identifying the focus of their learning
- Want a role in deciding how things are done in their own classroom and perhaps in the school
- Want a supervisor who is knowledgeable about teaching and learning and is skilled at collaboration and coaching

I Think I've Figured Out A New Way To...

- Review alternatives and make rapid decisions about what to do
- May need help in finding resources to implement new initiatives
- View supervisor as a colleague engaged in the pursuit of increased student learning
- Want a supervisor who is respectful of their knowledge and skills, who listens well, who asks hard questions, and provides resources through coaching or access to materials and ideas

Supervisory and Mentoring Conference
Communication Skills

If You Want to Signal That You Are Ready to Concentrate & Listen
- Be prepared for the conference with notes analyzed, connections to past experiences clarified, and questions and discussion points ready
- Have calls held and cell phone off
- Put away all other papers that might be a distraction
- Make eye contact
- Nod affirmatively and make minimal encouraging responses like "I see", "Hmmm", "Interesting"
- Paraphrase what is said
- Avoid communication stoppers like "If I were you, I would have tried...", "Based on my experience, I feel that the best thing to do is...", "I told you that wouldn't work".

If You Want to Signal That You Want to Work Collaboratively...
Do all of the above and...
- Sit beside the teacher rather than behind a desk
- Meet in the teacher's classroom, workroom, or a neutral space rather than in an administrative office or conference room
- Provide the teacher copies of any notes you took during an observation prior to the conference
- Provide a copy of the questions you might be asking during the conference so that the teacher knows the level of thinking she/he will be asked to do
- Prepare copies of any materials you are going to refer to during the conference

If You Want to Signal...
- That the conversation is over...look at your watch, stand up and head toward the door
- That you are just going through the paces ...follow only your own script and do not respond to the teacher's silences, emotions, questions, and concerns; take phone calls, leave your cell phone on, have difficulty finding your observation notes or the draft of your report
- That you are taking a position of authority and/or superiority ...sit behind a desk
- That you have better things to do...flip through your calendar, make notes about unrelated issues...Teachers are really good at reading upside down!
- That you do not believe the supervision and evaluation process provides a valuable opportunity for professional dialogue...skip the conversations and conferences altogether and put the report in the teacher's mailbox!

Words of Wisdom on Conferencing...

Much has been written about approaches to conferencing. While a variety of terms has been used to describe conference approaches, an examination of several approaches reveals that they are far more alike than they are different. This review is provided so that readers can be comfortable with the use of consulting, collaborating, and coaching as the terms used to describe approaches to conferencing in the 21st Century.

Glickman, Gordon and Ross-Gordon

Glickman, Gordon, and Ross-Gordon describe four approaches to conferencing and feedback:

- **Directive-Control**: the supervisor tells the teacher what to do
- **Directive-Informational**: the supervisor lists the options and asks for input from the teacher
- **Collaborative**: The supervisor and teacher work together to share information and options for actions and as partners make a plan
- **Nondirective**: The supervisor facilitates the teacher's thinking so that the teacher can make a plan for herself

They contend that the approach should be selected to match the teacher's level of development, expertise, and willingness to change.

Madeline Hunter

Hunter described five types of observation conferences by identifying the outcomes for teacher reflection and decision making:

- The teacher is able to identify teaching decisions and behaviors that promoted learning and explain why they worked. The teacher can explain the **rationale or research** for why it worked.
- The teacher considers **alternative teaching decisions** and behaviors that also would have promoted learning and is able to explain why that is so.
- The teacher is able to identify areas with which she/he is not satisfied and identify potential solutions for those issues. The teacher **uses data on student engagement and learning** to make decisions.
- The teacher is able to **identify next steps** in expanding and refining his/her repertoire.
- The teacher will be able to identify **alternative strategies** to substitute for those behaviors **identified by the observer as not productive**. Hopefully, the teacher also knows that teacher actions need to change.

Words of Wisdom on Conferencing...

Hershey and Blanchard

Hershey and Blanchard in *Situational Leadership* provide four approaches to promoting change in behavior based on the teacher's readiness and willingness to change:

Direct   Clearly communicate what change must be made, as well as the time lines for change. Almost always used when performance is below the district standards. Extensive follow-up to ensure follow-through is essential. **(Tell)**

Recommend   Clearly communicate the need to change or improve behavior or techniques, but allow flexibility for the teacher to select from the options presented by the supervisor or mentor. The need for change is strong and follow-up to ensure follow-through is important. **(Sell)**

Facilitate   Discuss possible changes, but leave the decision open. Usually used to promote teacher decision making and/or repertoire building. Follow-up is in the form of support and encouragement **(Participate)**

Delegate   Leave the decision about what to change up to the teacher. Provide support, feedback, and recognition. Typically used with highly skilled, knowledgeable, and reflective teachers. Follow-up is in the form of encouragement and support. **(Delegate)**

Costa and Garmston

Costa and Garmston suggest that we focus on teacher decision-making rather than always focusing on teacher behavior. The three goals of cognitive coaching are:

- **establishing and maintaining trust**
- **facilitating mutual learning**
- **enhancing growth toward holonomy (simultaneously autonomous and interdependent)**

To observe Art Costa, Bob Garmston, one of their consultant group members, or someone who has developed skills through the cognitive coaching workshops is an awe-inspiring experience. They have fine-tuned this important component of our repertoires to an extraordinary level. Learning and becoming skilled at the process is time-consuming and requires a strong commitment to the process.

Words of Wisdom on Conferencing...

Lipton and Wellman

Present a continuum of interactions:
- Consult
  - ▸ most directive interaction
  - ▸ provide information and expert counsel
  - ▸ balance support with challenge
  - ▸ offer options
- Collaborate
  - ▸ promote mutual learning
  - ▸ facilitate mutual growth
  - ▸ create mutual respect
- Coach
  - ▸ least directive stance
  - ▸ mediate thinking
  - ▸ nonjudgmental interactions
  - ▸ support
  - ▸ reflection and inquiry

Blase and Blase

Enumerate five conference strategies:
- make suggestions
  - ▸ listen before making suggestions
  - ▸ extend teacher's thinking
  - ▸ use examples and models
  - ▸ give teacher choice about which suggestion to implement
  - ▸ encourage teachers to take risks
  - ▸ give suggestions both orally and in writing
- give feedback
  - ▸ make feedback nonjudgmental/nonevaluative
  - ▸ include infrequent constructive criticism
  - ▸ use praise
  - ▸ use collaborative approach
  - ▸ be available for further discussion of feedback
  - ▸ include student learning and behavior
- model
- use inquiry and open-ended questions
- solicit teacher opinions

Putting It All Together for
Reflective Conferences

1. Never lose sight of the essential goal of all supervisory or mentoring conferences: **teacher growth and increased student learning** no matter how well things are going.

2. Decide on conference approaches based on the teacher's **attitude, skills, and knowledge** around the issues to be discussed. It is highly likely that more than one approach will be used in a conference.

3. Plan **agenda and questions** carefully so that the interactions move the teacher toward the goals of the conference. Avoid leading questions.

4. Be conscious of the **time available** for the conference and pace accordingly. Do not be drawn off track into interesting, and perhaps even important, conversations for which this is not the appropriate forum.

5. In all supervisory and mentoring conversations and conferences, use language from the **professional performance criteria** so that those criteria become part of the shared language.

6. Use coaching as the **default strategy**. Start with coaching and return to coaching whenever possible.

7. Tie **feedback** to teaching or content standards, previous conversations, or staff development offerings.

8. Use **student work, student achievement data, or data** gathered from multiple sources to support question selection, opinions, suggestions, or directives.

9. Check for **understanding, agreement, and commitment**.

10. **Follow-up and follow-through.** Check to see if the agreements reached and the commitments made result in action. Follow-through by providing the resources and support promised.

11. Avoid **communication stoppers!**

12. Match style and word choice to the teacher's **information processing style**.

13. Use **feedback, encouragement, and praise** appropriately.

See Tool-19: Data Driven Discussions Format A - Focus on Teacher Behavior

See Tool-20: Data Driven Discussions Format B - Focus on Student Learning/Behavior

See Tool-21: Data Analysis Using ASK Construct

Consulting, Collaborating, and Coaching

Coaching and mentoring involve a variety of strategies that fall along a continuum. When partners use **consultation** strategies, one partner is the expert giving advice to the other (learner). In **collaboration,** both partners share expert and learner roles. **Coaching,** through questioning, facilitates thinking, planning, and reflecting around classroom practice.

Supervising, Coaching, & Mentoring Approaches	Consultation ◀■▶	Collaboration ◀■▶	Coaching ◀■▶
Purpose	Give advice to... • clarify goals • plan for, observe, and provide feedback about teaching practice • improve teaching practice • create resources • provide follow-up	Plan, observe, provide feedback, and refine instructional strategies to... • expand the knowledge base of both partners • improve practice and student learning results • share resources and expertise • develop collegial, professional relationships and diminish professional isolation	Use strategies to help a colleague think about and reflect on professional work as the individual shapes and reshapes his or her teaching practices and solves related problems.
Roles	A teacher or administrator who... • provides formal or informal opportunities to observe professional practice • clarifies problems and successes • gives advice regarding solutions, resources, or changes in practice when needed	Colleagues who... • enter a partnership targeting areas of their practices for examination and then providing and receiving feedback • collaborate as critical friends to improve teaching, student learning, and leading	A teacher or administrator who... • asks insightful questions to coach a partner's decision-making and reflective process • helps a colleague examine the relationship between perceptions, attitudes, thinking, and behaviors that will affect student learning
Knowledge & Skills	The supervisor, coach, or mentor... • is a skillful teacher or administrator • is able to describe or demonstrate effective teaching/administrative strategies • has a thorough understanding of the curriculum being taught • practices good listening and communication skills • is sensitive to other's needs • is effective in establishing rapport	The collaborative partners... • plan for and focus on developing skills and/or improving practice • practice good listening and communication strategies • are sensitive to each other's needs • are open to observation of and feedback on their teaching practice • are effective in establishing rapport	The supervisor, coach, or mentor... • is a good role model • is effective in establishing rapport • practices good listening and communication strategies • asks appropriate questions

Adapted from Results-Based Professional Development Models, St. Vrain Valley School District, Longmont, CO

Coaching Approach

Outcomes

The teacher becomes more reflective, more aware of the cause and effect of behaviors, and more conscious of the decision-making process used

Coaching Behaviors

- pause, paraphrase, and probe
- actively listen (See **Communication Strategies for Coaching** on page 192.)
- be non-judgmental
- encourage self-awareness
- encourage self-reflection
- use data, as appropriate
- See question stems on page 193.

When Used

- The teacher has the **knowledge, skills, and attitudes** to think through the decision making process, and, with coaching, arrive at own conclusions about what needs to be done.

- **This is the DEFAULT approach**! Start with coaching and return to coaching whenever possible!

Communication Strategies for Coaching

Attentive Silence

This adult **wait time** allows both parties to process what has been said, to collect their thoughts, to review notes, and to figure out and formulate next points of discussion.

Acknowledgment Responses

These responses are given to indicate that you are paying attention to what is being said. They are accompanied by head nodding, eye contact, and a posture matched to that of the teacher. When talking with a very reflective teacher, the vast majority of your responses may be acknowledgment responses. Interestingly enough, when the conversation or conference is over, the teacher may well say, "Thank you for your help," because what she needed to do was think out loud. Examples of acknowledgment responses are: **"I see." "That's interesting." "Hmmm."**

Paraphrasing and Summarizing

When paraphrasing, you check for understanding and summarize what the teacher said. You attempt to capture the essence of the feelings and content of the statement and paraphrase them in an abbreviated form. You make no inferences. In order to avoid adding your own voice, think of paraphrasing and summarizing as a parallel to the way you paraphrase to be sure you have the correct directions to a party.

Reflecting Meaning and Feelings

With this strategy, you add inferences about what you think the teacher is saying. For example, a teacher might say, "That lesson was a big success. The kids really got it!" You might respond, "You are feeling pretty good about the learning results you got!" If you are on the mark, the teacher response might be, "Yes! They did so much better than they have before!" If you are off the mark, the teacher might respond, "No, but they at least knew what to do." You make an effort to ensure you are interpreting the right emotion and that the words you heard conveyed the meaning the person meant to send.

Questions That Promote Teacher Thinking*

Costa and Garmston write that when you coach, you attempt to move the teacher with whom you are working to a new place. Carefully crafted questions can help you do that. Examples of such questions which are likely to promote teacher thinking are found on the next page.

*Costa and Garmston identify pause, paraphrase, and probe as the three essential skills of cognitive coaching.

Getting Started with
Questions That Promote Teacher Thinking

Questions that promote teacher thinking are open-ended; there is not one correct answer. They are not leading, accusatory, or nosy. We ask these questions to:

- **initiate a discussion and keep discussions on track**
- **focus on new concepts or a different aspect of a concept**
- **facilitate flexible thinking**
- **challenge the obvious**
- **break down complex tasks and issues**
- **consolidate previous discussions and experiences**
- **explore possible next steps**

Questions/Question Starters

- What do you need to do next?
- Based on what you know, what can you predict about ...?
- Does what ... said make you think differently about ...?
- How do you decide...?
- How does ... tie in with what we have discussed before?
- Suppose ..., what then?
- How does this match what you thought you knew?
- What might happen if ...?
- When have you done something like this before?
- What sort of impact do you think...?
- How would you feel if...?
- How did you come to that conclusion?
- How about...? What if...?
- Tell me what you mean when you...
- What do you think causes ...?
- When is another time you need to...?
- What do you think the variables/issues/problems are?
- What were you thinking when...?
- Can you think of another way you could do this?
- Why is this one better than that one?
- How can you find out?
- How is ... different (like) ...?
- What have you heard about..?
- Can you tell me more?
- What else do you see?
- How does that compare with...?

Reflective Conference Menus

Marcia Baldanza, Principal of Patrick Henry Elementary School, Alexandria, Virginia, created menus for the reflective conferences she holds with teachers. She shares the questions with teachers in advance so that they know the level of thinking they will be asked to do.

The questions included in Reflective Conference A begin quite analytically and move to more reflective thinking. Reflective Conference B is more reflective and begins to focus on asking for data to support opinions. Reflective Conference C is more data driven, and Reflective Conference D is designed to be used at the end of the year.

Reflective Conference A
- How did you decide what to teach today?
- How does what you and your students worked on today fit in the context of the unit on which you are working?
- How did you go about finding out if your students had the background knowledge and skills required to be successful on this lesson?
- How did you decide what instructional strategies to use today?
- What are the variables, beyond completion of assignments, that you consider in determining whether or not the students have learned what you wanted them to learn?
- What do you think worked and did not work in this lesson? Why do you say that?
- When you teach this lesson again, what will you do differently?

Reflective Conference B
- As you look back on this lesson, how do you think it went? What happened to make you think this way?
- What do you remember about your actions during the lesson? How did what you actually did match what you had planned? Why do you think that is the case?
- What do you remember about student work and behavior during the lesson? How did their actions and work match what you hoped/expected would happen?
- How successful were the students in moving toward competency with the standard? What is your data?
- What do you think caused some students to not "get it"?
- What did you notice that caused you to...?
- What did you learn from this conversation that may influence your future thinking and planning?

Reflective Conference Menus

Reflective Conference C

- From your perspective, was the learning objective clear and significant? What evidence can you provide?
- What percentage of the students mastered the objective? What evidence can you provide?
- What work did the students do to achieve the objective, and did that work add up to a quality learning experience? How do you measure that?
- To what extent were the students actively involved in the construction of meaning? What evidence can you provide?
- How do you explain students' success or lack of success?
- How will your practice change as a result of our reflection together?

Reflective Conference D

- As you examine data and look for trends, do your students typically have difficulty with the same areas or experience success in the same areas? In what areas? Why do you think that is so?
- Where would you like to see improvement?
- How closely did the students' products/performances match your expectations?
- What do you do to keep growing professionally?
- What do you need to do more of to keep growing professionally?
- How have you engaged in learning within the school?
- What strengths do you see in your practice?
- What areas for improvement can you identify?
- What experiences shape you as an educator?
- In what situations do you feel most/least competent?

Collaborative Approach

Outcome

Mutually agree on the next steps in learning or refining a new technique, identify problems, and develop solutions for problems

Collaborative Behavior

- focus on the teacher's agenda
- guide problem solving process
- explore pros and cons of solutions
- keep discussion focused on problem solving

When Used

The supervisor, mentor, or coach and the teacher are equally engaged in determining the next steps. The teacher has a positive **attitude** about his own capacity and the capacity of his students and, while knowledgeable and skillful, seeks to have even more **knowledge** and develop more **skills**.

Essential Components of the Collaborative Approach

- Identify the problem, issue, or concern from the teacher's perspective through sharing of data and questioning
- Check for understanding of the issues
- Brainstorm possible solutions
- Weigh alternatives
- Agree on a plan and a follow-up meeting to assess if solution is working and plan next steps

See the next page for a description of the **Six Step Problem Solving Process** that is widely used for individual and group problem solving.

Skills for Collaborative Problem Solving

- pausing, paraphrasing, and probing
- active listening
- "I-messages" or assertive messages
- brainstorming
- consensus building

For information on these prerequisite skills, see **People Skills** by Robert Bolton.

The Six-Step Problem Solving Method

Step One: Identify the Problem

A great deal of time is spent solving the wrong problem. Often people try to "fix" a symptom rather than getting to the problem. Once the problem can be written in a problem statement that says, "The problem is that...", write a goal statement describing what a successful remedy would accomplish. It may be that the problem is so big and complex that the components of the problem may need to be tackled one at a time.

Step Two: Generate Potential Solutions

This step calls for divergent thinking and brainstorming. The goal is to generate as many potential solutions as possible. Consider doing individual brainstorming before you share ideas. Do not judge solutions as they are generated, but jot them down for later consideration as a solution or as a component of the solution. Do not stop too soon. Often the best ideas come toward the end of the brainstorming because ideas begin to be integrated.

Step Three: Evaluate the Solutions

Some suggested solutions may need to be eliminated because of the time, energy, or money they would require. Others may be eliminated because of policies and rules. After those have been eliminated, examine the remaining possibilities and rank order them by criteria you design. Identify the two or three solutions that have the best potential and analyze them further as to how feasible it would be to implement them and the possible impact each might have.

Step Four: Select a Solution to Try

In this step the teacher decides which solution to try. If the solution involves the assistance of other people, they will need to be consulted about their willingness to participate. Once a solution is identified, decide on the criteria to be used to evaluate the effectiveness of the solution after the implementation.

Step Five: Make a Plan and Implement It

Using the description of the ideal situation, the solution selected to try, the time frame for implementation, and the criteria to be used to evaluate the effectiveness of the solution, make an action plan and implement it.

Step Six: Evaluate the Solution

Use the criteria established in step five to decide whether or not the solution is working and determine if the plan should be modified. Use the problem solving process to plan any needed modifications.

Consulting Approach

Outcomes

The teacher:
- learns new techniques
- perfects a technique
- changes a behavior
- develops a plan for change
- determines next steps

Consultant Behaviors

- pause, paraphrase, and probe
- inform
- direct
- model
- give advice
- critique
- make suggestions
- give instruction for change
- Glickman, Gordon, and Ross-Gordon identify two consultant options
  - supervisor tells the teacher what to do
  - supervisor lists options and asks the teacher to chose from those options

When Used

The supervisor, mentor, or coach has a predetermined notion of what should happen and believes that the teacher does not have, in the moment, the knowledge, skills, or attitudes to determine what needs to be done.
It may be that the teacher:
- does **not have knowledge** about the topic under discussion
- is **not skilled** at identifying and solving problems
- has **little commitment** to teaching or student learning
- is doing something that is potentially harmful to students

Difficult Conferences

No one likes to deliver bad news and few relish the need to help a staff member develop a new picture of his/her own performance and its impact on student learning. Doing this, however, is one of the responsibilities held by supervisors, evaluators, and, in some instances, mentors.

Careful planning of these difficult interactions is essential. In many difficult conferences, whether or not the conference is a formal part of the supervisory process, there are additional people present. This might include parents, students, colleagues, or association representatives. It is important to consider the role each plays.

Peggy McNeil McMullen provides an excellent framework for identifying the issues we should think about before, during, and after difficult conferences.

Begin with the End in Mind

Prepare in advance by identifying for yourself the outcomes you want to achieve, as well as the messages you want to convey.

Be realistic in setting the agenda. Rather than planning to bring up multiple issues, focus on what is both doable and would make the most difference in terms of teacher performance and student learning.

Prepare written "talking points" so that you can check back through them as the conference progresses.

Outline agenda to include "If this, then...".

Gather appropriate documents and have available copies as needed.

As appropriate, provide participants information prior to the conference so they can be better prepared to participate in the conference.

Communicate Information Clearly

Present the agenda and the purposes at the beginning of the meeting.

Establish time frame of meeting.

Tell the person your concerns and feelings directly. Do not "sugar coat," but also do not bring up unrelated issues.

Refer to examples, quotes, or data of some form to illustrate your concerns.

Consider the quality, intensity, and/or frequency of the problem as you explain your concerns.

Difficult Conferences

Stay Flexible

Within the boundaries of your goals and beliefs, consider alternative explanations or solutions.

Be willing to discuss other interpretations of what you see as a problem or negative pattern.

Move into a problem solving mode when appropriate. See the six step problem solving process on page 197.

Focus on the Needs of the Child

Do not lose sight of the fact that you must be focused on what's best for the child's learning and emotional needs.

Acknowledge Contributions/Strengths as Well as Areas of Growth/Improvement

Acknowledge positive contributions, assets, skills, and motives of the teacher/parent/child so it's clear that the focus is on behavior and not a general attack on him/her as a person.

This is a particularly important one if the conference is with a teacher who contributes in powerful ways to the social and/or extracurricular systems in the school, but whose classroom performance does not meet standards. While we want to acknowledge those "beyond the classroom" contributions, we have to be clear that without the classroom performance, they are insufficient.

Include All Participants

Ensure that all participants feel included in the conference and have ample opportunity to express their views.

Include introductions as appropriate.

Check for understanding, agreement, and/or commitment frequently across all participants.

Respond with Calm

Show emotion only in a controlled way.

Do not get defensive or "hooked."

Understand that others may get emotional and that crying may be essential to moving toward resolution. Be kind but focused.

Difficult Conferences

Respond with Calm continued...

If the emotions of others get out of hand, terminate the conference and reschedule.

Listen

Listen as objectively as possible.

Watch the non-verbal behavior and listen to the language used by others and match your own language and response to the exhibited information processing and communication styles (i.e., I feel/I think, analytical/global, intraverted/extraverted).

Pay attention to attributions. When others make external attributions respond with, "Given that you see it that way, how might you/we ...?"

Pause, probe, and paraphrase.

Tolerate silence.

Resist using the communication road blocks.

Refocus

Refocus discussion to the outcomes you identified if and when the talk moves off target for an extended period.

Acknowledge the importance of the issue or point that is a distraction and state that while it is important/interesting, this is not the correct forum or time to discuss that issue.

While allowing for input and differing viewpoints, be sure that agenda items are addressed.

Plan Follow-Up

Summarize key points.

Specify the next steps.

Articulate expected actions and time lines for action as well as the support systems that will be provided by you or the school system.

Check for understanding, agreement, and commitment to both the key points and the next steps.

If there are consequences for lack of follow through, identify the consequences.

Set a date and time for another meeting if necessary.

Difficult Conferences

Document

Create a written report of the conference.

Distribute it to all participants and other appropriate personnel.

Analyze and Reflect

Consider how what happened during the process matched what you wanted to happen.

Do a mental cause and effect analysis.

Make a mental list of what you would do differently next time.

Take any additional action you may need to take based on the match between desired and actual outcomes.

After a Difficult Conference...

When all is said and done, we can control only one person's behavior...our own. Whether the conference was focused on instruction, professional behavior, or parent issues, as we analyze and reflect on how it went, our own behavior is where we begin. Administrators in Leading the Learning workshops suggest that we consider the following variables:

- I was appropriately honest. I carefully identified the issues that had to be surfaced.
- I supported what I said with data.
- I actively listened.
- I was clear and direct.
- I provided constructive suggestions for improvement.
- I gave the person the opportunity to reflect and return to talk with me.
- I owned the critical comments that I made.
- I was fair, respectful, courteous and confidential.
- I expressed support and worked to identify ways to improve the situation.
- I checked for understanding.
- I summarized and put the summary of the conference and any agreements in writing, if appropriate.
- I was organized, prepared, and rehearsed for both the cognitive and affective parts of the conference. I prepared "if this happens, then I will say ..." statements.
- I remained calm.
- I didn't get emotionally "hooked" or sidetracked by extraneous issues.
- I did not take ownership of "stuff" that wasn't mine.
- I believed and articulated expectations that change could occur.
- I maintained dignity and integrity.

● I did it in the best interests of the students.

Written Observation Reports

Given that many contracts currently require written observation reports, how do we write reports in a way that clearly communicates that:

- it's what happens after the teacher stops talking that counts
- student learning is the goal
- student work and student achievement data guide our decisions

yet gives us time to have those productive conversations with teachers?

Three Approaches for Written Observation Reports

We base our write-ups on **student work, observations of student work habits, and on other available data that provides evidence of student learning**. We then make inferences about what teacher decision making and/or actions led to those student results.

and/or

We write **generalizations about observable teacher behavior** based on the district teacher performance criteria and support the significance of that behavior by describing the behavior's impact on student learning or research findings about best practice.

and/or

We use the **constructs of attitudes, skills and knowledge** about/with content, learners, and repertoire as they result in student learning to identify areas for reinforcement, refinement, or reflection.

See Tool-19: Focus on Teacher Behavior

See Tool-20: Focus Student Learning/Behavior

See Tool-21: Data Analysis Using ASK Construct

Formal Observation Reports

Fairfax County Public Schools (FCPS), Fairfax, Virginia, for many years used an observation report format developed by Jon Saphier of Research for Better Teaching. When contracts or situations call for implementation of traditional observation cycles, this is far and away the best approach to use in preparing observation reports.

The FCPS report included three sections. They were the Lesson Overview, Standards of Performance Observed, and a Diagnostic Focus. The **Lesson Overview** described the context in which the observation was conducted. This included a brief description of the overall lesson, the timing, the composition of the class, and any significant influences impacting the teaching and learning situation. The second section, **Standards of Performance Observed,** addressed performance indicators observed and the specific evidence or data gathered to support the claim that the indicator occurred. Additionally, mention was made of the impact of the teacher behavior on student learning. The last section was originally entitled **Areas for Improvement or Growth** and later called **Diagnostic Focus**. The purpose of the section remained the same in that it focused attention on the next steps. Each report was to have entries in each of the three sections.

While this format is an excellent one, it could be enhanced by including in the Lesson Overview the standards of learning on which the lesson was focused. It could be further enhanced by the inclusion of reflective questions in the Diagnostic Focus.

Additionally, when permissible by contract, the written observation report's value would increase if it included information from the planning conference and was not written in final form until after the reflective conference. This would create an opportunity to portray a fuller picture of the teacher's decision-making process. When key points from the reflective conference are also included in the report, the teacher's thinking could be extended and captured for both parties to recall.

Writing these reports is a time-consuming process. It is essential that the observer identify truly significant events and patterns of behavior/decision making to include in the report. Interviews with teachers indicate that it is the conversations about the observation and the report that promote the most growth. Interviews with supervisors indicate that they spend so much time writing the reports that they do not have sufficient time to have in-depth discussions with teachers about the teaching and learning episodes. The reality is that conversation and conference agendas should be carefully constructed to include the same components as the written reports.

Mind Your Words!

When you want to say that the decision making, behaviors, and results exceed expectations, use:

initiates

creates

selects and adapts

capitalizes

encourages

interrelates

integrates

enhances

discovers

mentors

seeks out

modifies

conceptualizes

leads

innovates

collaborates

develops

delegates

supervises

coordinates

synthesizes

When you want to say that the decision making, behaviors, and results are on target, use:

demonstrates

recognizes

establishes

selects

matches

implements

maintains

organizes

applies

prepares

promotes

follows

manages

monitors

exhibits

participates

serves

utilizes

When you want to say that the decision making, behaviors, and results do not meet standards, use:

contradicts

misconstrues

misinterprets

is inconsistent

is inaccurate

is inappropriate

does not

misses opportunities

is unclear

is insensitive

does not use data

does not exhibit

does not participate

lacks

ignores

neglects

is unclear

inadequate

rarely

seldom

Hard to Measure Words

These words, which are frequently found in criteria, rubrics, and in write-ups, often cause confusion instead of opportunities for growth because they lack specificity and measurability:

- appropriate/inappropriate
- understands
- effective/ineffective
- consistently/inconsistently
- generally
- occasionally/rarely

Defining Quality and Quantity

In an effort to provide clarity, the Texas Professional Development and Appraisal System describes these hard to measure words in the following way:

Quality is represented by strength, impact, variety, and alignment

- **Strength:** depth of knowledge, knowledge of complexity or conceptual foundation
- **Impact:** promotes student success, productive, promotes student responsibility, challenging, promotes reflection
- **Variety:** appropriate to meet the varied characteristics of students, promotes engagement/learning, appropriate to the lesson objective, multidimensional
- **Alignment:** connection to a set of objectives and expectations external to the classroom, congruency, progression, leads to understanding of unified whole, appropriate to varied characteristics of students, relevant

Quantity is represented by frequency counts/percentage of time or repeated evidence

- **Frequency counts** are difficult to measure but are better quantified by percentage of time such as 90-100% of time for all/almost, 80-89% of the time for most, 50-79% of that time for some, and 49% or less for less than half of the time.
- **Repeated evidence:**
  - Consistently: Uniformly, see it from the beginning to the end, highly predictable, routines are seamless
  - Generally: Common practice, predictable, typically prevalent, as a rule
  - Occasionally: sporadic, random, moderately, more often than not, irregular
  - Rarely: infrequent, nonexistent, not attempted, minimal, hardly, no/none

Quality, Intensity and Frequency

When deciding whether the overall teaching performance meets or exceeds standards, or in some cases, does not meet standards, the constructs of quality, intensity, and frequency are useful tools to use in the analysis of performance with quality being the starting point of the analysis.

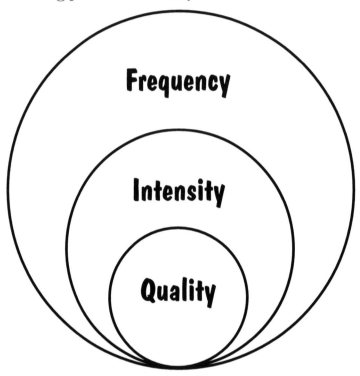

Quality

How well is the behavior done?
How well is it matched to the standards, the students, the situation?
Quality is communicated through words such as:
- involves/encourages students
- accommodates differences
- interrelates
- creates, innovates
- reassesses and modifies
- matches
- presents inaccurate information
- misses opportunities
- incorrectly

Quality

How well is the behavior done?

How well is it matched to the standards, the students, the situation?

Quality is communicated through words such as:

- involves/encourages students
- accommodates differences
- interrelates
- creates, innovates
- reassesses and modifies
- matches
- presents inaccurate information
- misses opportunities
- incorrectly

Intensity

What is the level of involvement?

What is the strength of the commitment?

What is the depth of the participation?

Intensity is communicated through words such as:

- initiates
- creates
- stimulates
- seeks out opportunities
- collaborates
- shares
- is a resource
- takes little or no responsibility
- does not participate

Frequency

How often is it done?

Frequency is communicated through words such as:

- seamlessly
- consistently
- frequently
- often
- always
- inconsistently
- rarely

Efforts must be taken to clarify or quantify words describing frequency.

The Commonwealth of Massachusetts Department of Education's Evaluation Procedures and

Sample Observation Report

Teacher: Ms. M

Planning Conference: February 8, 2003

Observation Date: February 9, 2003

Reflective Conference: February 13, 2003

Report Date: February 14, 2003

Context

The 45 minute observation period included the last 15 minutes of a writing lesson and 30 minutes of a social studies lesson. There were 25 students, including four inclusion students and three ESL students in the class.

Standards Addressed

> The fifth grade writing standards (benchmarks, indicators, etc.) being addressed in this lesson were:
>
> a.
>
> b.
>
> c.
>
> The fifth grade social studies standards (benchmarks, indicators, etc.) being addressed in this lesson were:
>
> a.
>
> b.

Significant Observations

A comparison of the baseline data on student achievement and the targets Ms. M set for her fifth grade learners as they progress toward mastery of grade level benchmarks reveals a strong focus on, and solid student progress in, writing and in using cause and effect to interpret social science issues. For example... (data cited for high achievers as well as struggling learners, inclusion and ESL students).

The planning and pacing guides Ms. M used to orchestrate the learning experiences, observed during the February 9th observation, reveal the use of both criterion-referenced data and anecdotal records to make instruction decisions about how to group the students for the day's writing lesson and to select materials for the whole class social studies lesson. For example, she and the students did an error analysis of their last few writing assignments and used that data to organize focus groups. As we watched the students finish their writing focus groups, Ms. M indicated that when she listened in on small work groups last week, many students were still struggling with clearly identifying cause and effect connections and, therefore, she decided to engage the entire class in a follow-up social studies lesson designed to help students clarify their thinking on cause and effect using a variety of print sources.

Students are encouraged to take responsibility for monitoring their work. Students told me during the observation that in addition to keeping interactive notebooks, they are asked daily to assess their own learning and the effectiveness of their work habits in their journals. A brief review of five interactive notebooks (3 general, 1 inclusion, and 1 ESL) provided data that even students who entered the class with learning challenges or deficiencies in their writing are building skills in both narrative and expository writing and in the use of graphic organizers to decode text structures.

Several visual surveys of the classroom revealed that all students engaged in the learning process during the Think-Pair-Shares and, with limited teacher prompting, during the focus group peer editing using a posted format. All but one student (not inclusion or ESL) moved age appropriately to designated areas of the room and followed directions without needing to ask for clarification. The one student responded to a quiet comment from Ms. M and after two false starts, settled into the work in progress.

Next Steps
In the follow-up conference, Ms. M indicated an interest in and plans for organizing a vertical team to analyze when and how students are introduced to, instructed in the use of, and asked to independently use text structure as they move through their school years.

Teacher Signature_____

Observer Signature_____

Areas for Improvement or Growth
Making Suggestions and Giving Directives

Many districts not only require written observation reports, they also require that all observation reports include suggestions. These suggestions may be for improvement or growth. The language used in this section of observation reports signals how much latitude the teacher has in taking the action cited in the suggestion.

Suggestions for Growth (optional)

Consider
Consider alternative strategies
A way to enhance
I encourage you to
Continue to
Continue to investigate
I challenge you to
Possibilities include
Explores
Share

Directives for Improvement (nonnegotiable)

Do not allow
Must
Ensure that
Should
It is important to
Implementing ... is essential
... needs to be the starting point
I am very concerned
It needs to be
It is essential
It is imperative
In order to meet district standards, you must
Improvement must be made
You need to establish
You need to incorporate
I would encourage you to
It is strongly recommended
Implement the following
decrease ... and increase ...

Tie all suggestions and directives to data gathered from multiple sources, to the research on best practice, and/or to district standards.

Evaluation Report Example A

Teacher: Molly Master

School: Sequoyah Elementary School

Teaching Assignment: Special Education

School Year: 2003-2004

Date of Report: April 15, 2003

Ms. Master has made the potentially difficult transition from functioning as a "pullout" special educator to one who co-teaches in a blended classroom smoothly and skillfully. This is evidenced through walkthroughs as well as through conversations with Molly, her co-teachers, and parents. In conferences with parents and in planning sessions with colleagues, she purposefully and thoughtfully brings her knowledge of human development, learning theory, and the learning and behavioral characteristics of special needs students to the surface and ensures that they are integrated into the instructional design and, as appropriate, incorporated into suggestions to parents on ways to support learning at home.

A review of student records and student work indicates that Ms. Master not only blends IEP objectives with established standards and benchmarks, she also helps general education teachers support special needs students without lowering expectations for their capacity to learn at high levels.

As we have discussed, future areas of professional growth focus include continuing to build her skills at organizing productive learning environments when the class size is much larger than she has experienced in the past. Additionally, Molly plans to concentrate on expanding her knowledge and understanding of the science standards and curriculum. There are logical next steps in which she can seek the advice and council of her general education colleagues, as well as take advantage of professional development offerings in the district.

These areas of focus and skill development Molly has identified can only add to the expertise she provides at Sequoyah Elementary School.

Evaluation Report Example B

Example of text for a summative evaluation report when there has been frequent ongoing discussions between the teacher and the supervisor, as well as many opportunities for the two to collaboratively analyze, reflect, and respond to data. As Tom Garcia, Assistant Superintendent for Human Resources, St. Vrain Valley School District, Longmont, Colorado, says, "The hard work went on during the year rather than when the evaluator sat down at the computer to write the report."

Terry Teacher, history and social sciences teacher at Will Rogers High School, consistently demonstrates his commitment to being a standards-based teacher, to the achievement of high standards by all students, and to the support of district goals.

A review of teacher artifacts includes a year-long curriculum map and pacing guide, unit plans, and classroom summative assessments provide evidence that he used district standards and the standards-based planning process to plan for the year, for units, and for daily lessons.

Mr. Teacher integrates literacy, numeracy, and technology into his social studies instructional program. The use of new skills and knowledge he gained through participation in a study group on reading in the content areas and through enrollment in a graduate level course on instructional technology is evident during walkthroughs and in the comments/suggestions he makes during team and department meetings. Of particular note is his tenacity in seeking out resources and materials to better integrate numeracy with social studies curriculum.

The professional growth goals Terry established for this year have led him to model and promote the concepts of developing common assessments and looking at student work to determine the effectiveness of staff efforts. While his work has led to implementation by some members of the department, he considers this to be a "work in progress" and plans to continue his work on this goal during the next school year.

As an accomplished classroom teacher, Mr. T skillfully organized a productive and positive learning environment in US History classes. As a result of the changing demographics in our district, his new challenges are scaffolding instruction and sheltering English for second language learners. This will be his new professional growth focus for the next school year.

Evaluation Report Example C

Teacher: Melissa Messner

School: Martin School

Teaching Assignment: 5th Grade Language Arts

School Year: 2003-2004

Date of Report: April 15, 2004

Ms. Messner is in her sixth year of teaching at Martin School. During the school year there were three rounds of the formal observation process, numerous walk-throughs, as well as reviews of student work and teacher records.

As evidenced in the attached observation reports and summaries of other conferences, the following pattern of decision-making and performance has evolved:

Planning: Despite the fact that she has been provided the district outcomes, a curriculum map developed by teammates, teacher resource materials to support programs identified as closely aligned with district outcomes, and professional development opportunities focused on planning, Ms. Messner has not yet demonstrated that she can independently plan instruction using the standards-based process. She continues to use lesson plans that were designed prior to the implementation of our current district standards.

Instruction: When provided direct assistance, Ms. Messner co-designs standards-based lessons; however, as cited in each of the observation reports, in the classroom she asks primarily lower level questions that are not aligned with the level of thinking required by the standards. When using teacher resource materials that accompany district adopted reading materials, she selects the questions that can be answered with one or two-word answers.

Assessment: An analysis of Ms. Messner's classroom assessment results reveals that her students are unable to apply classroom lessons to new situations in appropriate ways. The review of student work indicates that while they can recall facts in isolation and outline steps in processes, they are unable to interpret and analyze readings or successfully apply the processes in their own writing.

For in-depth information on supervising and evaluating teachers who do not meet standards, see *The Skillful Leader* by Andy Platt and Caroline Tripp.

Environment: Ms. Messner has an organized and tidy classroom. All materials are stored in easily accessible and well labeled locations. Routines and procedures are announced, modeled, practiced, and followed by students. Students arrive in class with all their materials, move quickly to their seats, and begin work. There are no organizational issues. The special needs students in the classroom are able to follow the clearly outlined behavioral expectations.

This orderly environment provides a setting in which students should be able to do rigorous work. They are not routinely asked to do so. Discussions with Ms. Messner reveal that she thinks that it is more important for students to feel good about themselves than it is for them to be challenged intellectually. As stated earlier, she can, with guidance, plan more rigorous instruction. She needs to demonstrate that she can consistently plan and implement rigorous instruction and to become comfortable with students who are not always successful on the first attempt.

Professionalism and Collegial Collaboration: Ms. Messner is punctual in attendance and in filing all required documents. She attends all required meetings and participates actively in those meetings. She serves on the social committee and plans the annual end of year staff social event.

Ms. Messner indicates that she is willing to work with colleagues to learn from them and that she is willing to work hard to master the content and the planning process. Despite this professed willingness to work hard and improve, little change in practice was evidenced this year. An improvement plan will be designed and an intervention team will work with Ms. Messner during the 2003-2004 school year.

For indepth information on supervising and evaluating teachers who do not meet standards, see *The Skillful Leader* by Andy Platt and Caroline Tripp.

Improvement Plan

Name: Melissa Messner
School: Martin School
Teaching Assignment: 5th Grade Language Arts
School Year: 2003-2004
Date of Report: May 15th, 2004

Areas of Concern

- Planning Instruction
- Implementing instruction
- Assessing Learning and the Instructional Program

Goals

- Use the SBE Planning Process to design units and lessons aligned with district standards
- Provide a more rigorous instructional program by designing and using tasks and questions aligned with the district outcomes that are written at higher levels of thinking; use Bloom's Taxonomy as a tool
- Ensure that organizational systems are developed and used in the interest of student learning rather than simply for management
- Use district rubric to assess student writing

Strategies

- Meet with an intervention team member twice a month to review and preview plans for instruction, how actual outcomes match desired outcomes, and plan revisions.
- Use the curriculum map designed by team members to chunk instruction for the year. Submit three to four page outline for the year by September 1st, 2004.
- Submit daily lesson plans to your supervisor on Friday for the following week. While there may be scheduling adjustments, materials, learning tasks, and focus questions to be used are to be identified.
- Enroll in Instruction for All Students offered by the Office of Professional Development, and complete all assignments.
- Observe at least three other teachers with the same teaching assignments, and one teacher who teaches fourth grade for the purpose of comparing the rigor of the student work. Teachers to be observed will be identified in collaboration with your supervisor.
- Participate in team scoring of student work using the district writing rubric.

Resources

- Intervention Team
- Supervisor to accompany you on at least one observation
- Instruction for All Students workshop series and assignment review
- Four observed teachers
- Lesson plans review by supervisor and intervention team member

Review Dates

- September 1, 2004: Outline of the year
- Weekly, beginning 1st week of school: Weekly lesson plans
- Peer Observations: One each quarter to be discussed with supervisor within week of each observation
- Assignments from Instruction for All Students: Day before next workshop session with supervisor
- Regular evaluation cycle components

Leading the Learning
Tools

Tools
Collaboration Tools
Data Gathering Tools
Data Analysis Tools
Feedback Tools
Instructional Planning Tools

This section includes thumbnails of reproducible tools for supervisors, mentors, coaches, and teachers to use in their efforts to maximize their efforts to increase students achievement. Full-size templates can be found on the CD-ROM located in a pocket attached to the inside back cover of this text.

See the CD-ROM Table of Contents on pages 221-222.

These tools may be reproduced for use within your school or school district. All other uses, including commercial use, is prohibited without written permission of Just ASK Publications.

Leading the Learning Tools
CD-ROM Table of Contents

Leading the Learning Tools
CD-ROM Table of Contents

Instructional Planning Tools

Leading the Learning Tools

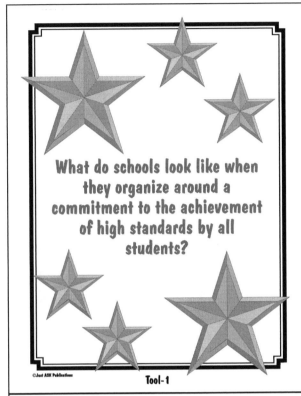

What do schools look like when they organize around a commitment to the achievement of high standards by all students?

Tool-1

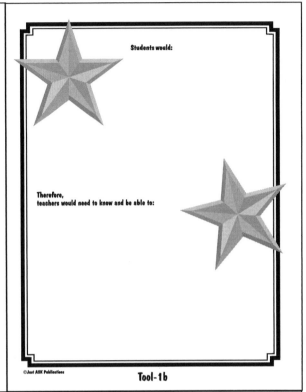

Students would:

Therefore,
teachers would need to know and be able to:

©Just ASK Publications

Tool-1b

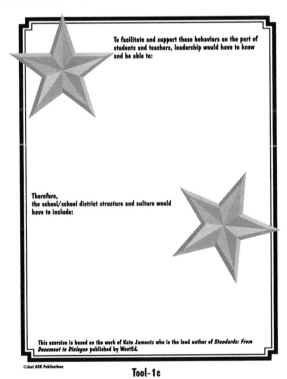

To facilitate and support those behaviors on the part of students and teachers, leadership would have to know and be able to:

Therefore,
the school/school district structure and culture would have to include:

This exercise is based on the work of Kate Jamentz who is the lead author of *Standards: From Document to Dialogue* published by WestEd.

©Just ASK Publications

Tool-1c

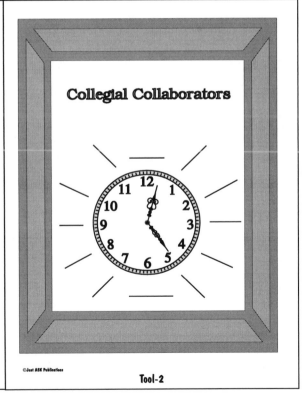

Collegial Collaborators

©Just ASK Publications

Tool-2

Leading the Learning Tools

My Frame of Reference for...

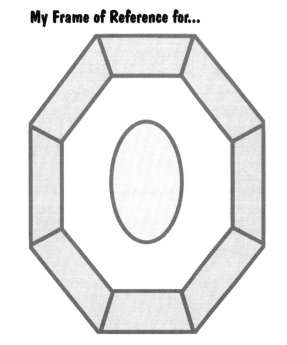

©Just ASK Publications   Tool-3

If _____ was happening in the classroom, we would

See	Hear

©Just ASK Publications   Tool-4

Stir the Faculty on:

1 Your own idea

2 Your own idea

★ 3 Your own really original idea!

4
5
6
7
8
9
10
11
12
13
14
15
16
17
18
19
20

©Just ASK Publications   Tool-5

Data Analysis and Integration

We use data to:	Skillful Use	Learning to Use	Need to Learn
• build a body of evidence to include classroom, district, state, and national data			
• improve the instructional program			
• provide teachers feedback on the effects of their efforts			
• provide students feedback on their performance			
• develop a common understanding of what quality student performance is and how close we are to achieving it			
• measure program results, efficiency, and cost effectiveness			
• understand if what we are doing is making a difference over time by tracking students			
• understand if what we are doing is making a difference over time by examining programs, curriculums, and departments			
• ensure that students/groups of students "do not fall through the cracks" by disaggregating the data in multiple ways			
• identify cause and effect relationships			
• guide curriculum development, integration, and revision			
• develop School Improvement Plans			
• design professional development plans			
• meet district, state, and federal requirements			

©Just ASK Publications   Tool-6

Leading the Learning Tools

Collegial Collaboration
Practices That Promote School Success

We are educators who use our knowledge, skills, and energy to...	Frequently	Sometimes	Rarely
• analyze standards, and design instruction and assessments to match those standards			
• design and prepare instructional materials together			
• design and evaluate units together...especially those based on clearly articulated national, state, or local standards			
• research materials, instructional strategies, content specific methodologies and curriculum ideas to both experiment with and share with colleagues			
• design lesson plans together (both within and across grade levels and disciplines)			
• discuss/reflect on lesson plans prior to and following the lesson			
• examine student work together to check match to high standards and to refine assignments			
• agree to experiment with an idea or approach, to debrief about how it worked, and to analyze the results and make adaptations and adjustments for future instruction			
• observe and be observed by other teachers			
• analyze practices and their productivity			
• promote the concepts of repertoire and reflection			
• teach each other in informal settings and in focus groups			
• use meeting time for discussions about teaching and learning rather than administrivia			
• talk openly and often about what we are learning or would like to learn			
• concentrate efforts and dialogue on quality and quantity of student learning, rather than on how many chapters have been covered in the text			

Tool-7

Three Column Chart...

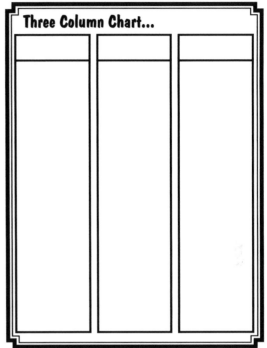

Tool-8

3:
2:
1.

Tool-9

Scavenger Hunt
Instruction for All Students

Page references are for *Instruction for All Students* Second Edition.

1. Find someone who has used several different ways to **CHECK FOR STUDENT UNDERSTANDING**. Have her explain what she did, why she did it, and what the impact was on learning. **Book References: pages 89 and 154-156.**

2. Find someone who can explain the rationale for and the sequence of planning in the **SBE PLANNING PROCESS** (Think four steps!) and can truthfully say that he is getting really comfortable with **"BEGINNING WITH THE END IN MIND!"** **Book References: pages 31-54.**

3. Find someone who can explain **RAFT** and can describe one she has used in her instructional program. Also have her explain why the idea of **RAFT** is an important one. **Book References: pages 135-139 and 189-194.**

Tool-10

Leading the Learning Tools

Scavenger Hunt continued...

4. Find someone who sees the connection between **DIFFERENTIATED INSTRUCTION AND HIGH STANDARDS FOR ALL STUDENTS**. Ask him to explain why the two are **THE PERFECT PAIR**. **Book References: pages 195-216.**

5. Find someone who can explain the difference between a **RUBRIC** and a **PERFORMANCE TASK LIST** and can further explain the advantages and disadvantages of each. Also have her share how she goes about designing or selecting rubrics and performance task lists. **Book References: pages 175-180.**

6. Find someone who can explain the importance of surfacing and dealing with **STUDENT MISCONCEPTIONS**. Have that person share a few bits of his repertoire for surfacing misconceptions. **Book References: pages 57-61, 91, 101-102, and 109-114.**

Tool-10b

Scavenger Hunt continued...

7. Find someone who used a new **ACTIVE LEARNING** strategy within the past month. Have him describe the activity and its impact on learning. **Book References: pages 83-120.**

8. Find someone who can briefly explain how she has refined her use of the **LECTURE**. Ask her to explain how she has gone about integrating that refinement into her ongoing practice. **Book References: pages 65-72.**

9. Find someone who uses the gifts of Mary Budd Rowe. Have him explain **10:2 THEORY** and **WAIT TIME** and how the use of those strategies has positively impacted the learning environment in his classroom. **Book References: pages 87 and 263-264.**

Tool-10c

Scavenger Hunt continued...

10. Find someone who can explain how she has refined her use of **DISCUSSIONS** and the impact that has had on student learning. **Book References: pages 73-77.**

11. Find someone who can explain what it means to **FRAME THE LEARNING** and is purposeful about doing so each day in his classroom. Have him describe the process he uses. **Book References: pages 57-62.**

12. Find someone who can identify the variables of **MULTIPLE INTELLIGENCES THEORY** and then explain how he has integrated their use into the planning of instruction. **Book References: pages 50 and 127-132.**

Tool-10d

Scavenger Hunt continued...

13. Find someone who has seen positive results from having and **COMMUNICATING** to students explicit **STANDARDS** and **CRITERIA** for **ASSESSMENT**. Have her explain exactly what has happened or is happening. **Book References: pages 58-59.**

14. Find someone who can explain the components of **BLOOM'S TAXONOMY**, has used the taxonomy to analyze standards and district outcomes, and has developed expertise in using it to design questions or tasks for her students. **Book References: 231-235.**

15. Find someone who can explain **TASK ANALYSIS** and its role in the SBE Planning process. **Book References: pages 38, 40, and 46-47.**

Tool-10e

Leading the Learning Tools

Interview Questions about "The Way We Do Business Around Here in a Standards-Based Environment"

1. What exactly do you mean when you say that you work in a school/district that is committed to the **achievement of high standards by all students?**

2. What would I have seen you and your colleagues doing during the last school year that was **different from what I would have seen six years ago?**

3. There has been a great deal written lately about **"data-driven" decisions.** How does that play out in your day-to-day work? How about in the day-to-day work of teachers?

4. How has this **emphasis on data affected the discussions** you have with colleagues?

Tool-11

Questions about "The Way We Do Business Around Here" continued...

5. Given the high visibility, accountability and pressure all educators face today, how do you **support colleagues, teachers, and learners?** Please share some examples.

6. How about some examples of **support that you have received from your colleagues,** your staff, and those who supervise you?

7. When staff or colleagues say there are just too many demands coming from too many directions, how do you respond in a way that helps them understand **the connectedness of all the initiatives?**

8. What have you found effective in dealing with **stakeholders who say** that standards are taking all of the creativity and spontaneity out of teaching and learning?

Tool-11b

Questions about "The Way We Do Business Around Here" continued...

9. Given that high achievement by all students absolutely calls for **collegial collaboration,** how have you modeled and supported it?

10. How have the educators with whom you work dealt with the construct that **expectations are the same for all students,** even those who in the past have not been expected to perform at high levels?

11. How has the **teacher supervision and evaluation system** been impacted by the standards-based movement?

12. How has **administrator supervision and evaluation** been impacted by the standards-based movement?

Tool-11c

Questions about "The Way We Do Business Around Here" continued...

13. How have school staffs from buildings across the district worked together to ensure **continuity and to maximize efforts** across the district? (This might include vertical and horizontal teams across and between buildings or curriculum mapping, as well as informal and formal interactions between grade level teams and departments.)

14. Given that all the literature includes references to **professional development and to job-embedded learning,** how has your practice and your priorities around those aspects of professional life changed? That is, what have you given up so that you and your staff/colleagues can make time for professional learning communities?

15. What do you think **parents and community members** would have noticed about the differences in the "way you are doing business?" What evidence causes you to think this?

16. And, the bottom line question... What would **the students** with whom you work most closely have to **say about** all this emphasis on high achievement? What would those students who have not previously been held accountable in such a way have to say?

Tool-11d

Leading the Learning Tools

Now Hear This!

The Education News Flash focus this hour is on the work at/in

_____

as reported by_____.

The notable accomplishment/effort in the interest in high achievement by all students is:

Now Hear This!

The Education News Flash focus this hour is on the work at/in

_____

as reported by_____.

The notable accomplishment/effort in the interest in high achievement by all students is:

Tool-12

Peer Observation Request

Name_____ Date_____

On which standards/benchmark will you focus? _____
_____

What is the skill/lesson you want to improve? _____
_____

Who do you want to observe and why? _____
_____

How does this observation connect to your professional development goal?
_____
_____
_____
_____

	Name of person to observe	Date	Time
1st Choice	_____	_____	_____
2nd Choice	_____	_____	_____

Signature _____ Signature of Observee_____

Administrator's Signature _____

Tool-13

Peer Poaching Pass!

_____visited my class on _____ so that she/he could learn how to further the learning of more students more of the time.

Signed_____

Peer Poaching Pass!

_____visited my class on _____ so that she/he could learn how to further the learning of more students more of the time.

Signed_____

Peer Poaching Pass!

_____visited my class on _____ so that she/he could learn how to further the learning of more students more of the time.

Signed_____

Peer Poaching Pass!

_____visited my class on _____ so that she/he could learn how to further the learning of more students more of the time.

Signed_____

Peer Poaching Pass!

_____visited my class on _____ so that she/he could learn how to further the learning of more students more of the time.

Signed_____

Peer Poaching Pass!

_____visited my class on _____ so that she/he could learn how to further the learning of more students more of the time.

Signed_____

Peer Poaching Pass!

_____visited my class on _____ so that she/he could learn how to further the learning of more students more of the time.

Signed_____

Peer Poaching Pass!

_____visited my class on _____ so that she/he could learn how to further the learning of more students more of the time.

Signed_____

Tool-14

Providing Context for Formal Observations

Please complete this form and submit it the day before we hold our planning conference. This information will provide context for our conference and the upcoming observation. Thank you in advance for the time it will take you to complete this form. Having this information will enable us to ensure that the time we spend together promotes both your growth and student learning.

Teacher_____ Grade/Subject_____ Date_____

Overview: Please provide any information you think is essential for my understanding of the context in which this lesson occurs.

What do you expect students to know and be able to do at the end of this lesson? How does this relate to unit outcomes and district/state standards, benchmarks, and indicators?

How will you and the learners assess the learning? Please include both formative and summative assessment plans. Please attach a copy of the summative assessment and the assessment criteria.

Tool-15

Leading the Learning Tools

What are the learning experiences in which the students will be engaged? How/why did you select these learning experiences?

What instructional materials and resources will be used? How did you identify those materials?

What difficulties do you think might interfere with student learning? What have you planned proactively to minimize or eliminate those problems?

What organizational systems are in place to facilitate student learning? How well are these systems working for you and the learners?

Tool-15b

To:

From:

Date:

During my visit I noticed...

To:

From:

Date:

During my visit I noticed...

Tool-16

Walk-Through Observations and Feedback

Teacher's Name _____

Date _____

Subject/Grade _____

Focus of Walk-Through (Optional) _____

Standards/Indicators being addressed:

Students were:

Teacher was:

Evidence of rigor:

Evidence of positive and productive environment:

Points to Ponder:

Tool-17

Whole School Observation Form

Use this form to capture data about the implementation of the best practices you see across the school or throughout a department or grade level. Use the district's performance criteria or strategies the staff is studying together as the focus of the data gathering. You can provide feedback electronically or in a newsletter.

Teacher Name	A	B	C	D	Data

In the areas designated A, B, C, and D insert the the specific behaviors for which you are observing on a given day. You may choose to observe for only one or two at a time. In the "DATA" column include teacher actions, student actions, and artifacts.

Tool-18

Leading the Learning Tools

Notes for Data Driven-Discussions of Teaching and Learning

Performance Indicator/Teacher Behavior noted:

Data:

Data:

Impact on Student Learning:

Performance Indicator/Teacher Behavior noted:

Data:

Data:

Impact on Student Learning:

Performance Indicator/Teacher Behavior noted:

Data:

Data:

Impact on Student Learning:

Performance Indicator/Teacher Behavior noted:

Data:

Data:

Impact on Student Learning:

Performance Indicator/Teacher Behavior noted:

Data:

Data:

Impact on Student Learning:

Performance Indicator/Teacher Behavior noted:

Data:

Data:

Impact on Student Learning:

©Just ASK Publications

Tool-19   Format A: Focus on Teacher Behavior

Notes for Data Driven-Discussions of Teaching and Learning

Student Learning/Behavior Noted:

Performance Indicators/Teacher Behavior(s) which promoted student learning:

Student Learning/Behavior Noted:

Performance Indicators/Teacher Behavior(s) which promoted student learning:

Student Learning/Behavior Noted:

Performance Indicators/Teacher Behavior(s) which promoted student learning:

Student Learning/Behavior Noted:

Performance Indicators/Teacher Behavior(s) which promoted student learning:

Student Learning/Behavior Noted:

Performance Indicators/Teacher Behavior(s) which promoted student learning:

Student Learning/Behavior Noted:

Performance Indicators/Teacher Behavior(s) which promoted student learning:

©Just ASK Publications

Tool-20   Format B: Focus on Student Learning/Behavior

Data Analysis Using ASK Construct

	Content	Learners	Repertoire
Attitudes			
Skills			
Knowledge			

©Just ASK Publications

Tool-21

Observation Conference Feedback

Please complete this form and return it to me. Your reactions and analysis will be helpful to me as I constantly work to improve my conferencing skills.

Key: 1 = Strongly Agree   2 = Agree   3 = Disagree

During the conference, you:

1.	Clearly communicated the purpose of the conference	1	2	3
2.	Involved me in the discussion	1	2	3
3.	Listened well throughout the conference	1	2	3
4.	Exhibited positive non-verbal language	1	2	3
5.	Provided specific feedback about my performance	1	2	3
6.	Checked to see if feedback (or suggestions) was clear to me	1	2	3
7.	Helped me to analyze my performance	1	2	3
8.	Encouraged or allowed me to express my opinions	1	2	3
9.	Helped me reflect on what I do	1	2	3
10.	Were tactful, yet task-oriented	1	2	3
12.	Provided suggestions or offered to help if asked	1	2	3
13.	Helped me consider different strategies or approaches	1	2	3
14.	Reinforced what I did well	1	2	3
15.	Focused on important aspects of teaching	1	2	3

Adapted from the NASSP Practitioner, October, 1989

©Just ASK Publications

Tool-22

Leading the Learning Tools

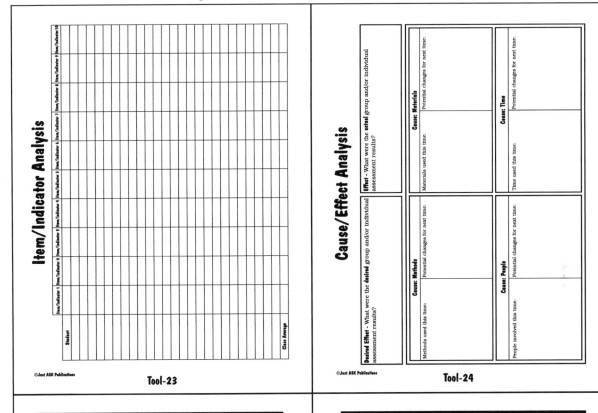

Item/Indicator Analysis

Student

Item/Indicator 1 Item/Indicator 2 Item/Indicator 3 Item/Indicator 4 Item/Indicator 5 Item/Indicator 6 Item/Indicator 7 Item/Indicator 8 Item/Indicator 9 Item/Indicator 10

Class Average

©Just ASK Publications
Tool-23

Cause/Effect Analysis

Desired Effect - What were the **desired** group and/or individual assessment results?

Effect - What were the **actual** group and/or individual assessment results?

Cause: Methods
Methods used this time:
Potential changes for next time:

Cause: Materials
Materials used this time:
Potential changes for next time:

Cause: People
People involved this time:
Potential changes for next time:

Cause: Time
Time used this time:
Potential changes for next time:

©Just ASK Publications
Tool-24

Attitudes, Skills, and Knowledge Goal Setting

A _____
_____

S _____
_____

K _____
_____

©Just ASK Publications
Tool-25

Improvement of Student Achievement Plan

Teacher_____
Grade/Subject_____
School_____

Area of Focus:

Baseline Data:

Goal Statement/Target:

Action Plan/Strategies to be Used:

Signatures and Date_____

©Just ASK Publications
Tool-26

Leading the Learning Tools

Tool-26b

Mid-Year Review of Plan Implementation:

Interim Achievement Data:

Signatures and Date_____
End-of-the Year Analysis of Plan Implementation:

Achievement Data:

Next Steps:

Signatures and Date_____

Student Impact Plan

Reflection Questions

What do I need to do to keep developing professionally?

How could I grow professionally to meet the needs of my students?

How could I engage in learning within my school setting?

How will I identify goals that are critical to my professional growth and to student learning?

How can I further building and district goals?

In what areas do I feel most or least competent?

In what areas do my students excel?

In what areas do my students struggle?

What can I do differently that will affect those areas in which my students struggle?

Section I: Data Collection
What data did you collect and examine?

What does the data suggest?

Strengths:

Area(s) for improvement:

Other questions:

Additional data:

Section II: Goal(s) Development
Goal Statement:

Identify the domain(s) for this goal.

How does your goal link to your building NCA target goals?

How does your goal link to the district's strategic goals?

How does your goal link to improving student achievement?

Tool-27

Student Impact Plan

Reflection Questions

How does this student impact plan link to what I already know?

Why am I considering this particular plan?

What resources do I need for this plan and how can they be obtained?

How does this plan relate to other learning activities I intend to pursue?

How comfortable will I be engaging in this plan?

What will be the easiest and most difficult parts of this plan?

How will I change as a result of this plan?

Will this plan foster collegiality?

How can I link this plan to the work of my colleagues?

How can my plan benefit my colleagues?

Whom can I call upon for feedback?

What evidence of my learning will I produce?

What will I observe, count, or measure to determine whether the changes in practice as a result of this plan have improved student learning?

How long will it be before improvement can be measured?

Section III: Plan
What specific activities will you undertake that will help you to achieve your goal?

What is the timeline for working on this goal?

What resources do you need to help you achieve your goal?

What criteria will you use to assess the effectiveness of your student impact plan?

Identify the type of your student impact plan.

____ Individual
____ Collaborative
____ Building/Department
____ District-wide

If your plan is collaborative, building/department, or district-wide, identify the other teacher(s) with whom you will be working.

Date _____   **Teacher's Signature** _____

Date _____   **Supervisor's Signature** _____

Tool-27b

Student Impact Plan

Reflection Questions

What did I do for this plan?

What did others do for this plan?

How did the anticipated plan compare to how it actually went? What went as I planned and what did not?

What have I learned from this plan?

What new questions do I have as a result of this plan?

What am I doing differently in my teaching and learning practice as a result of this plan?

What are my students doing differently as a result of this plan?

What do I want to do now?

With whom do I want to share the results of this plan? How and when do I do that?

Section IV: Reflection

What has worked well in your plan to achieve your goal? Why?

What has not worked well in your plan to achieve your goal? Why?

Have you achieved your goal? If so, what evidence reflects your achievement? If not, what evidence reflects that and what do you do now?

As a result of your work toward this goal, do you need to continue work in this area or are you ready to put closure on it? Why?

Date _____   **Teacher's Signature** _____

Date _____   **Supervisor's Signature** _____

Developed by the Supervisory Process Team, District #220, Barrington, IL

Tool-27c

Leading the Learning Tools

Year End Reflections

Please respond to the following questions. You may attach additional pages as necessary. Return to me by the end of the day on _____.
Your responses may be typewritten or handwritten.

Name_____ Date_____

1. What "worked" in your classroom this year? Please provide examples (i.e. instructional strategies, learning activities, assessments, organizational strategies, etc.).

2. What did you want to be "better" at doing in the beginning of the year?

Jessica Overboe, Skyline High School, St. Vrain Valley School District, Longmont, CO

Tool-28

---

3. What did you get "better" at this year?

4. What didn't work in your classroom this year? What changes will you make for next year?

5. What data sources did you use this year to alter or analyze your instruction and your students learning?

6. In what ways could I have been more helpful to you in the role of evaluator?

©Just ASK Publications

Tool-28b

Interactions around Teaching and Learning

Teacher	Sept	Oct	Nov	Dec	Jan	Feb	March	April	May	June
Conversation / Walk Through / Observation / Conference										

©Just ASK Publications

Tool-29

Interview Questions for Teacher Positions

Here are questions and ideas or words to look for and listen for in the candidate's responses. Please score the candidate as follows:
1 - no skill, knowledge, understanding; **2** - some skill, knowledge, understanding;
3 - significant skill, knowledge, understanding.

Candidate:_____ **Interviewer:**_____

Planning Instruction
SBE evident in teaching, content knowledge, learning, and assessment; lesson design, talk of learning styles, brain research, diversity, active learning, connections, and integration.

- How do you translate "beginning with the end in mind" into planning and pacing for the year, the unit, and the lesson?

_____Score

Implementing Instruction
Framed learning, content knowledge, dealing with misconceptions, clear communication of purpose, expectations, directions, questions; making connections, ability to differentiate, accommodating and adapting; repertoire of strategies, materials, and resources.

- How do you frame the learning for students?

_____Score

- When and why do you ask questions of students?

_____Score

- Give examples of active learning strategies in your repertoire.

_____Score

©Just ASK Publications

Tool-30

©Just ASK Publications   233

Leading the Learning Tools

Tool-30b

Assessing Learning and the Instructional Program
Assessment continuum, content knowledge, checking for understanding; designing, selecting, and implementing paper-pencil tasks, performance assessments, rubrics; use of results to inform teaching decisions.

- How do you make sure students are ready to learn?

_____ Score

- How are you sure they're on the learning journey with you?

_____ Score

- How are you sure they caught what you just taught?

_____ Score

Orchestrating a Positive Learning Environment
Building a community of learners; having and communicating high expectations to all students; building capacity through learning how to learn; using errors and/or lack of background knowledge as learning opportunities; building reflection and metacognition; building appropriate and positive relationships with students.

- Define praise, encouragement, and feedback. How do you use them in a positive learning environment?

_____ Score

- What four qualities exist in a good place to learn?

_____ Score

©Just ASK Publications

Tool-30c

How do you deal with unmet expectations?

_____ Score

Leading a Learning-Centered Environment
Organizing systems for teachers, learners, and the classroom, reluctant or resistant learners; respect, dignity, consequences to match behavior; active learning, motivation, problem-solving, caring, fairness and respect; interaction with students; enthusiasm, motivation, dedication to teaching, reflective practice.

What is a learning-centered classroom and what do you do to create and lead in such an environment?

_____ Score

How do you get and keep students' attention?

_____ Score

Discuss classroom interior design.

_____ Score

How do you group students?

_____ Score

©Just ASK Publications

Tool-30d

Collaborating with Colleagues and Parents
Formats for collaboration: job-embedded professional development, coaching, mentoring, teaming; parents as partners.

- How do you build positive and productive relationships with parents?

_____ Score

- What does collaboration mean to you?

_____ Score

- Not all groups are teams. How will you know you're on a team, and not just a part of a group? What will you contribute to our teams?

_____ Score

RECOMMENDATION:

17-28	29-40	41-50
No Way!	Maybe...	Sign 'em up!

COMMENTS:

Marcia Baldanza, Principal, Patrick Henry Elementary School, Alexandria City Public Schools (ACS), Alexandria, VA

©Just ASK Publications

Tool-31

Improvement Plan

Name:

School:

Subject/Grade:

Area(s) of Focus:
        (Write out complete performance indicator or standard to be addressed.)
-
-
-

Teacher Behaviors/Actions to be Demonstrated/Evidenced:
-
-
-
-

Strategies/Action Plan:
-
-
-
-
-

Resources/Support Systems:
-
-
-
-

Review Dates:

Signatures and Dates

_____

©Just ASK Publications

Leading the Learning Tools

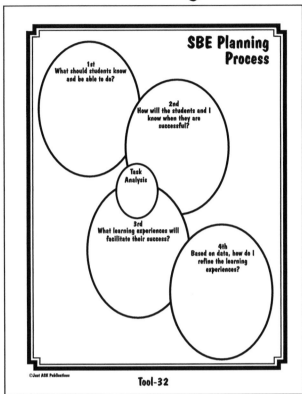

SBE Planning Process

1st
What should students know and be able to do?

2nd
How will the students and I know when they are successful?

Task Analysis

3rd
What learning experiences will facilitate their success?

4th
Based on data, how do I refine the learning experiences?

©Just ASK Publications

Tool-32

Unit Title_____ Unit Designer_____

Use this form is designed to help supervisors and peers do a quick review of a unit to ensure that all essential components are present. Use back for additional comments and suggestions.

Essential understandings are identified and aligned with standards, benchmarks, and indicators (List on back.)
1.
2.
3.

Summative assessment reflects CRAVE...coherency, rigor, authenticity, validity, and engagement
1. Coherency
2. Rigor
3. Authenticity
4. Validity
5. Engagement

Task analysis identifies knowledge, skills, and level of understanding needed for success
1. Knowledge
2. Skills
3. Level of Understanding

Learning experiences are congruent with identified standards, essential understanding, summative assessment, and task analysis
1.
2.
3.
4.
5.
6.
7.
8.
9.

Multiple pathways to success are provided through differentiation of instruction
1.
2.
3.

©Just ASK Publications

Tool-33

Unit Plan A

Unit of Study:

Standards:

Essential Questions/Key Ideas/Concepts:

Assessment Strategies
  Preassessment:

  Formative:

  Summative: (What criteria?)

Possible Learning Experiences/Assignments:

Materials and Resources Needed:

©Just ASK Publications

Tool-34

Unit Plan B

UNIT TITLE:		LEVEL:
STANDARDS BEING ADDRESSED:	PREVIOUS UNIT(S):	
	FOLLOW-UP UNIT(S):	
KEY/ESSENTIAL QUESTIONS:	SUMMATIVE ASSESSMENT(S):	

MAP OF THE UNIT: SEQUENCE OF EVENTS/LESSONS	TIME ALLOCATION:

©Just ASK Publications

Tool-35

Leading the Learning Tools

UNIT PLAN B: PAGE 2

MATERIALS/RESOURCES:	TECHNOLOGY RESOURCES:
VOCABULARY:	DIFFERENTIATION:
INSTRUCTIONAL STRATEGIES (include literacy strategies):	FORMATIVE ASSESSMENT STRATEGIES:

©Just ASK Publications

Tool-35b

Lesson Planning Guide

State or District Standards Being Addressed:	Essential Understandings:
	Summative Assessment(s):
Instructional Strategies:	Assignments/Learning Tasks/Formative Assessment:

Issues to Consider in Lesson Planning

1. What new learning will occur in this lesson?
2. How will my students use/apply their knowledge in meaningful ways?
3. How will the information in this lesson connect to my students' prior knowledge?
4. How will the learning connect with my students' lives beyond the classroom?
5. How will I extend students thinking?
6. What resources/materials do I need to gather to provide multiple pathways to learning?
7. How will I let students know the learning outcomes and the assessment criteria?
8. How can I engage students in self-assessment and self-adjustment?

Adapted from Kathleen Waltz, West Irondequoit Central School District, Rochester, NY

©Just ASK Publications

Tool-36

Task Analysis

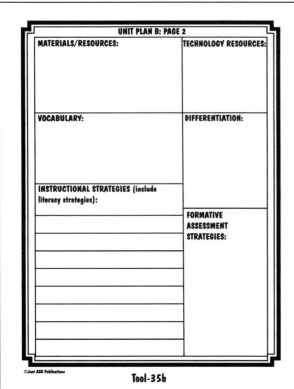

Knowledge	Skills

Knowledge	Skills

©Just ASK Publications

Tool-37

The TOP TEN QUESTIONS to ask myself as I design LESSONS

Page references are for *Instruction for All Students* Second Edition.

1ˢᵗ Oval

1. What should **students know and be able to do** as a result of this lesson? How are these objectives related to national, state, and/or district standards? How are these objectives related to the **big ideas/key concepts** of the course? Consult your state and district learning standards and your district curriculum for guidance with this question. See pages 43-45 in *Instruction for All Students* for information on big/ideas and key concepts.

2ⁿᵈ Oval

2. How will **students demonstrate what they know and what they can do**? What will be the **assessment criteria** and what form will it take? See pages 149-180 in *Instruction for All Students*.

©Just ASK Publications

Tool-38

Leading the Learning Tools

TOP TEN QUESTIONS CONTINUED...

3rd Oval: Questions 3 - 10 address the 3rd Oval.

3. How will I find out what students already know (**pre-assessment**), and how will I help them access what they know and have experienced both inside and outside the classroom? How will I help them **build on prior experiences, deal with misconceptions**, and re-frame their thinking when appropriate? See pages 83-120 in *Instruction for All Students*.

4. How will new knowledge, concepts, and skills be introduced? Given the **diversity of my students** and the **task analysis**, what are my **best options for sources and presentation modes**? See pages 55-82 in *Instruction for All Students*.

Tool-38b

TOP TEN QUESTIONS CONTINUED...

5. How will **I facilitate student processing (meaning making)** of new information or processes? What key questions, activities, and assignments (in class or homework) will promote understanding, retention, and transfer? See pages 121-148 in *Instruction for All Students*.

6. What shall I use as **formative assessments** or **checks for understanding** during the lesson? How can I use the **data** from those assessments to **inform my teaching decisions**? See pages 154-156 in *Instruction for All Students*.

7. What do I need to do to **scaffold instruction** so that the learning experiences are productive for all students? What are the multiple ways students can access information and then process and demonstrate their learning? See pages 195-216 in *Instruction for All Students*.

Tool-38c

TOP TEN QUESTIONS CONTINUED...

8. How will I **Frame the Learning** so that students know the objectives, the rationale for the objectives and activities, the directions and procedures, as well as the assessment criteria at the beginning of the learning process? See pages 57-62 in *Instruction for All Students*.

9. How will I build in opportunities for students to make **real world connections** and to learn and use the **rigorous and complex thinking skills** they need to succeed in the classroom and the world beyond? See pages 181-194 and 217-247 in *Instruction for All Students*.

10. What adjustments need to be made in the **learning environment** so that we can work and learn efficiently during this study? See pages 249-266 in *Instruction for All Students*.

Tool-38d

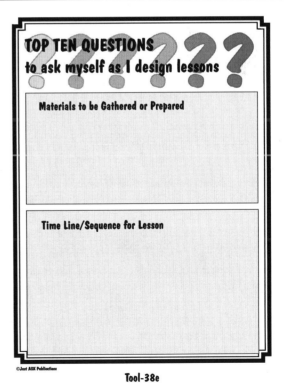

TOP TEN QUESTIONS
to ask myself as I design lessons

Materials to be Gathered or Prepared

Time Line/Sequence for Lesson

Tool-38e

Leading
the
Learning
Appendices

Instructional Resources and References

Allen, Janet. **Words, Word, Words: Teaching Vocabulary in Grades 4-12**. Portland, Maine: Stenhouse Publishers, 1999.

Armstrong, Thomas. **Multiple Intelligences in the Classroom**. Alexandria, VA: ASCD, 1994.

Beers, Kylene and Barbara Samuels. **IntoFocus: Understanding and Creating Middle School Readers**. Norwood, MA: Christopher-Gordon Publishers, Inc., 1998.

Benjamin, Amy. **Writing in the Content Areas**. Larchmont, NY: Eye on Education, 1999.

Bolton, Robert. **People Skills**. New York: Simon & Schuster, 1979.

Bowers, Bert, Jim Lobdell and Lee Swenson. **History Alive**! Menlo Park, CA: Addison-Wesley Publishing Company, 1994.

Burke, Kay. **What to Do with The Kid Who...** Arlington Heights, IL: Skylight Professional Development, 2000.*

Campbell, Linda, Bruce Campbell and Dee Dickinson. **Teaching and Learning Through Multiple Intelligences**. Needham Heights, MA: Allyn and Bacon, 1996.

Calkins, Lucy McCormick. **The Art of Teaching Reading**. New York: Longman, 2001.

Curwin, Richard and Mendler Allen. **Discipline with Dignity**. Alexandria, VA: ASCD, 1998.

Daniels, Harvey. **Literature Circles: Voice and Choice in the Student-Centered Classroom**. York, Maine: Stenhouse Publishers, 2002.

Dodd, Anne Wescott. "Engaging Students: What I Learned Along the Way." **Educational Leadership**. September 1995, pp 65-67.*

Educators in Connecticut's Pomeraug Regional School District 15. **Performance-Based Learning and Assessment**. Alexandria, VA: ASCD, 1996.

Faber, Adele and Elaine Mazlish. **How to Talk So Kids Will Listen and Listen So Kids Will Talk**. New York, NY: Avon, 1980.

Help! They Don't Speak English Starter Kit for Primary Teachers. Oneonta, NY: The Eastern Stream Center on Resources and Training (ESCORT), 1998.*

Gilbert, Judy, Editor, with the Centennial BOCES SBE Design Team. **Facilitator's Guide and Workbook: Common Ground in the Standards-Based Education Classroom**. Longmont, CO: Centennial BOCES, 1997.

Glasser, William. **Control Theory in the Classroom**. New York: Harper & Row, 1986.

Instructional Resources and References

Gordon, Thomas. **T.E.T. Teacher Effectiveness Training**. New York: David McKay Company, Inc, 1974.

Harvey, Stephanie and Anne Goudvis. **Strategies That Work**. Portland, Maine: Stenhouse Publishers, 2000.

Johnson, David. **Every Minute Counts: Making Your Math Class Work**. Palo Alto, CA: Dale Seymour Publications, 1982.*

_____ **Making Minutes Count Even More: A Sequel for Every Minute Counts**. Palo Alto, CA: Dale Seymour Publications, 1986.*

Joyce, Bruce and Marsha Weil. **Models of Teaching**. Boston MA: Allyn and Bacon, 1996.

Keene, Ellin Oliver and Susan Zimmermann. **Mosaic of Thought**. Portsmouth, NH: Heinemann, 1997.

Kohn, Alfie. **Beyond Discipline: From Compliance to Community**. Alexandria, VA: ASCD, 1996.

Kuzmich, Lin. **Data Driven Instruction Facilitator's Manual**. Longmont, CO: Centennial BOCES, 1998.

Lapp, Diane, James Flood and Nancy Farnan. **Content Area Reading and Learning Instructional Strategies**. Boston, MA: Allyn and Bacon, 1996.

Marzano, Robert J., Deborah Pickering, and Jane Pollack. **Classroom Instruction That Works: Research-based Strategies for Increasing Student Achievement**. Alexandria, VA: ASCD, 2001.*

Mendler, Allen. **Power Struggles: Successful Techniques for Educators**. Rochester, NY: Discipline Associates, 1997.

Putting Reading First. Center for the Improvement of Early Reading Achievement (CIERA). 2001.*

Rutherford, Paula. **Instruction for All Students**. Alexandria, VA: Just ASK Publications, 2008.*

Rutherford, Paula. **Why Didn't I Learn This in College?** Alexandria, VA: Just ASK Publications, 2009.*

Saphier, Jon and Robert Gower. **The Skillful Teacher**. Carlisle, MA: Research for Better Teaching, 1997.

Saphier, Jon and Mary Ann Haley: **Activators**. Carlisle, MA: Research for Better Teaching, 1993.

_____ **Summarizers**. Carlisle, MA: Research for Better Teaching, 1993.

Instructional Resources and References

Standards-Based Classroom Operator's Manual. Longmont, CO: Centennial BOCES, 2002.

Teague, Tori, Editor. **Standards-Based Classroom Operator's Manual, 3rd Edition**. Longmont, CO: Centennial BOCES, 2002.

Tomlinson, Carol Ann. "Reconcilable Differences? Standards-Based Teaching and Differentiation." **Educational Leadership**. Alexandria, VA: ASCD, September 2000, pp 6-13.*

Tomlinson, Carol Ann. **The Differentiated Classroom: Responding to the Needs of All Learners**. 1999.*

Tierney, Robert, John Readence and Ernest Dishner. **Reading Strategies and Practices**. Boston, MA: Allyn and Bacon, 1995.

Vacca, Richard and JoAnne Vacca. **Content Area Reading**. New York, NY: Longman, 1999.

Wiggins, Grant. "Feedback - How Learning Occurs." A Presentation from the 1997 AAHE Conference on Assessment and Quality. Pennington, NY: 1997.*

Wiggins, Grant and Jay McTighe. **Understanding by Design**. Alexandria, VA: ASCD, 1998.

Winebrenner, Susan. **Teaching Gifted Kids in the Regular Classroom**. Minneapolis, MN: Free Spirit, 1992.

Zemelman, Steven, Harvey Daniels and Arthur Hyde. **Best Practice: New Standards for Teaching and Learning in America's Schools**. Portsmouth, NH: Heinemann, 1998.

Entries marked with an asterisk (*) are recommended as texts for book clubs.

Process Resources and References

Airasian, Peter and Arlen Gullickson. **Teacher Self-Evaluation Tool Kit**. Thousand Oaks CA: Corwin Press, 1997.

Airasian, Peter, Arlen Gullickson, Lisa Hahn, and Dale Farland. **Teacher Self-Evaluation: The Literature in Perspective**. Kalamazoo, MI: Western Michigan University, Center for Research on Educational Accountability and Teacher Evaluation, 1995.

Blase, Jo and Joseph Blase. **Handbook of Instructional Leadership: How Really Good Principals Promote Teaching and Learning**. Thousand Oaks, CA: Corwin Press, 1998.

Bolton, Robert. **People Skills**. New York: Simon & Schuster, 1979.

Calhoun, Emily. "Action Research: Three Approaches." **Educational Leadership**. Vol 51 No. 2 1994, pp. 62-65.

Campbell, Dorothy, Pamela Bondi Cignietti, Beverly Melenyzer, Diane Hood Nettles and Richard Wyman. **How to Develop a Professional Portfolio**. Boston, MA: Allyn and Bacon, 1997.

California Standards for the Teaching Profession. Sacramento, CA: California Commission on Teacher Credentialing, California Department of Education, January 1997.

Content-Area Standards for Educators. Springfield, IL: Illinois State Board of Education, 2002.

Costa, Art and Robert Garmston. **Cognitive Coaching: A Foundation for Renaissance Schools**. Norwood, MA: Christopher Gordon, 1994.

Danielson, Charlotte. **Enhancing Professional Practice**. Alexandria, VA: ASCD, 1996.

Danielson, Charlotte. "New Trends in Teacher Evaluation." **Educational Leadership,** February 2001, pages 12-15.

Danielson, Charlotte and Thomas McGreal. **Teacher Evaluation to Enhance Professional Practice**. Alexandria, VA: ASCD, 2000.

DoDEA Educator Performance Appraisal Companion: DoDDS Edition. Arlington, VA: Department of Defense Education Activity, 2001.

DuFour, Rick and Richard Eaker. **Professional Learning Communities at Work**. Bloomington, IN: National Education Service, 1998.*

Process Resources and References

Essential Roles and Responsibilities within a Standards-Based Education System. SEB Design Team. Longmont, CO: Centennial BOCES, 1998.

Fink, Elaine and Lauren Resnick. "Developing Principals as Instructional Leaders" **Phi Delta Kappan**. April 2001, pp 598-606.

Gilbert, Judy, Editor, with the Centennial BOCES SBE Team. **Facilitator's Guide and Workbook: Common Ground in the Standards-Based Education Classroom**. Longmont, CO: Centennial BOCES, 1997.

Ginsberg, Margery and Damon Murphy. "How Walkthroughs Open Doors." **Educational Leadership**. May 2002, pp 34-36.

Glickman, Carl. **Leadership for Learning**. Alexandria, VA: ASCD, 2002.

_____ **Supervision of Instruction: A Developmental Approach**. Boston: Allyn and Bacon, 2001.

Glickman, Carl, Stephen Gordon and Jovita Ross-Gordon. **Supervision of Instruction: A Developmental Approach**. Boston, MA: Allyn & Bacon, 1998.

Graham, Beth and Kevin Fahey. "School Leaders Look At Student Work." **Educational Leadership**. March 1999, pp 25-27.

Guidelines for Performance-Based Teacher Evaluation. Missouri Department of Elementary and Secondary Education, 1999.

Guidelines for Uniform Performance Standards and Evaluation Criteria for Teachers, Administrators, and Superintendents. Richmond, VA: Division of Teacher Education and Licensure, Virginia Department of Education, 2000.

Hord, Shirley, William Rutherford, Leslie Huling-Austin, and Gene Hall. **Taking Charge of Change**. Alexandria, VA: ASCD, 1987.

Hunter, Madeline. "Six Types of Supervisory Conferences." **Educational Leadership**. 37(5), 1980, pp 408-412.

Igwanicki, Edward. "Focusing Teacher Evaluations on Student Learning." **Educational Leadership**. October 2001, pages 57-59.

Jamentz, Kate. **Standards: From Document to Dialogue**. San Francisco, CA: West Ed, 1998.

Process Resources and References

Kuzmich, Lin. **Data Driven Instruction Facilitator's Manual**. Longmont, CO: Centennial BOCES, 1998.

Lambert, Linda. "How to Build Leadership Capacity." **Educational Leadership**. April 1998, pp 17-19.

Laud, Leslie. "Changing the Way We Communicate." **Educational Leadership**. April 1998, pages 23-25.

Lipton, Laura and Bruce Wellman. **Mentoring Matters: A Practical Guide to Learning-Focused Relationships**. Sherman, CT: MiraVia, 2001.

Louis, Karen, and Sharon Kruse. **Professionalism and Community: Perspectives on Reforming Urban Schools**. Thousand Oaks, CA: Corwin Press, 1995.

Louis, Karen, Sharon Kruse, and Helen Marks. "Schoolwide Professional Community." **Authentic Achievement: Restructuring Schools for Intellectual Quality**. San Francisco, CA: Jossey-Basse, 1996.

McColskey, Wenda and Paula Egelson. **Designing Teacher Evaluation Systems that Support Professional Growth**. Greensboro, NC: SouthEastern Regional Vision for Education (SERVE), 1997.

 McKenna, Bernard, David Nevo, Daniel Stufflebeam, and Rebecca Thomas. **The School Professional's Guide to Improving Teacher Evaluation Systems**. Kalamazoo, MI: Center for Research on Educational Accountability and Teacher Evaluation, 1994.

Model Standards for Beginning Teacher Licensing and Development: A Resource for State Dialogue. Washington, DC: Interstate New Teacher Assessment and Support Consortium, Council of Chief State School Officers, 1992.

Model Standards for Licensing General and Special Education Teachers of Students with Disabilities: A Resource for State Dialogue. Washington, DC: Interstate New Teacher and Support Consortium, INTASC Special Education Sub-Committee, Council of Chief State School Officers Assessment, 2001.

Platt, Alexander, Caroline Tripp, Wayne Ogden, Robert Fraser. **The Skillful Leader: Confronting Mediocre Teaching**. Acton, MA: Ready About Press, 2000.

Peterson, Kenneth, Christine Wahiquist, Kathie Bone, Jackie Thompson, and Kay Chatterton. "Using More Data Sources to Evaluate Teachers." **Educational Leadership**. February 2001, pp 40-43.

Process Resources and References

Peterson, Kent and Terrence Deal. "How Leaders Influence the Culture of Schools" **Education Leadership**. September 1998, pp 28-30.

Practitioner: "The Supervisory Continuum: A Developmental Approach." Reston, VA: NASSP, October, 1995.

Professional Development and Appraisal System Participant's Manual. Austin, TX: Division of Educator Appraisal, Texas Education Agency, 1999.

Professional Performance Review. Greece, NY: Greece Central School District, 2000.

Results-Based Professional Development Models. Longmont, CO: Office of Professional Development, St. Vrain Valley School District, 2000.

Rutherford, Paula. **The 21st Century Mentor's Handbook**. Alexandria, VA: Just ASK Publications, 2005.*

Sagor, Richard. **Guiding School Improvement with Action Research**. Alexandria, VA: ASCD, 2000.*

Saphier, Jon. **How to Make Supervision and Evaluation Really Work**. Carlisle, MA: Research for Better Teaching, 1993.

Saphier, Jon and Matthew King. "Good Seeds Grow in Strong Cultures." **Educational Leadership**. March, 1985.

Sawyer, Lynn. "Revamping a Teacher Evaluation System." **Educational Leadership**. February 2001, pages 44-47.

Scriven, Michael, Pat Wheeler, and Geneva Haertel. **Teacher Evalaution Glossary**. Kalamazoo, MI: Sestern Michigan University, Center for Research on Educational Accountabiity and Teacher Evalaution, 1993.

Senge, Peter. **The Fifth Discipline: The Art and Practice of the Learning Organization**. New York: Currency Doubleday, 1990.

Shirnkfield, Anthony and Daniel Stufflebeam. **Teacher Evaluation: Guide to Effective Practice**. Boston MA: Kluwer Academic Publishers, 1995.

Schmoker, Mike. **Results**. Alexandria, VA: ASCD, 1996.*

Stanley, Sarah and W. James Popham, ed. **Teacher Evaluation: Six Prescriptions for Success**. Alexandria, VA: ASCD, 1998.

Process Resources and References

Stronge, James. **Qualities of Effective Teachers**. Alexandria, VA: ASCD, 2002.

Sullivan, Susan and Jeffery Glanz. **Supervision That Improves Teaching**. Thousand Oaks, CA: Corwin Press, 2000.

Supervisory Process. Barrington, IL: Barrington Community Unit School District 220, 2002.

Teacher Performance Evaluation Handbook. Fairfax County Public Schools Fairfax, VA: County School Board of Fairfax County, Virginia, 2002.

Teaching Matters: Strengthening Teacher Evaluation in Massachusetts. Monson, MA: MASSPARTNERS FOR PUBLIC SCHOOLS, 2002.

Teague, Tori, Editor. **Standards-Based Classroom Operator's Manual,** 3rd Edition. Longmont, CO: Centennial BOCES, 2002.

Warren-Little, Judith. "Norms of Collegiality and Experimentation: Workplace conditions of School Success." **American Educational Research Journal**. Fall 1982, Vol. 19, No. 3, pp 325-340.

Wiggins, Grant. "Feedback- How Learning Occurs." A Presentation from the 1997 AAHE Conference on Assessment and Quality. Pennington, NJ, 1997.*

Wolf, Dennie Palmer and Ann Marie White. "Charting the Course of Student Growth." **Educational Leadership**. February, 2000.

Entries marked with an asterisk (*) are recommended as texts for book clubs.

Index

Page numbers starting with Tool or Tools refer to pages located in the back of the book.

About the Author

Paula Rutherford is the author of multiple books including: ***Instruction for All Students***, ***Leading the Learning: A Field Guide for Supervision and Evaluation***, ***Meeting the Needs of Diverse Learners***, ***Why Didn't I Learn This in College?*** and ***The 21st Century Mentor's Handbook***. She writes an e-newsletter titled: ***Mentoring in the 21st Century®***.

Paula is president of Just ASK Publications & Professional Development, established in 1989 and based in Alexandria, Virginia. She works extensively with districts as they engage in long-term systemic work to align processes such as hiring, induction, professional development, school improvement plans, and supervision and evaluation. She also leads **Mentoring in the 21st Century® Institutes** across the country and has developed a comprehensive **Mentoring in the 21st Century® Resource Kit** so that districts can replicate the Just ASK institutes and provide extensive follow-up support for mentors. Paula, committed to building in-house capacity, has also developed a **New Teacher Professional Development Kit** that provides over 30 hours of support for new teachers and Certified Local Trainer (CLT) programs based on ***Instruction for All Students***, ***Leading the Learning***, and ***Why Didn't I Learn This in College?***

In addition to her extensive work as a consultant and trainer, Paula's professional experience includes work in regular education K-12 as a teacher of high school history and social sciences, physical education, Spanish, and kindergarten, as well as a special education teacher, coordinator of special education programs, administrator at the middle school and high school levels, and as a central office staff development specialist.

She can be reached at paula@justaskpublications.com.

Ordering Information

Books

Title	Order #	Price
Creating a Culture for Learning	11055	$ 34.95
Instruction for All Students	11027	$ 34.95
Instruction for All Students Facilitator's Handbook	11043	$ 59.95
Leading the Learning	11005	$ 34.95
Meeting the Needs of Diverse Learners	11033	$ 34.95
Meeting the Needs of Diverse Learners Facilitator's Handbook	11056	$ 74.95
Results-Based Professional Development Models	11058	$ 24.95
Standards-Based Classroom Operator's Manual	11012	$ 24.95
Strategies in Action: A Collection of Classroom Applications - Volume I	11049	$ 19.95
Strategies in Action: Applications in Today's Diverse Classrooms - Volume II	11054	$ 19.95
The 21st Century Mentor's Handbook	11003	$ 34.95
Why Didn't I Learn This in College? Second Edition	11002	$ 29.95
Why Didn't I Learn This in College? and *The 21st Century Mentor's Handbook* Save 20%	11029	$ 50.00

DVDs

Title	Order #	Price
Collegial Conversations	11031	$ 195.00
Helping New Teachers Succeed	11021	$ 60.00
Lesson Collection: Biology Visual Learning Tools (ASCD)	11026	$ 95.00
Lesson Collection: HS Geometry Surface Area and Volume (ASCD)	11034	$ 95.00
Lesson Collection: HS Reciprocal Teaching (ASCD)	11035	$ 95.00
Lesson Collection: Primary Math (ASCD)	11025	$ 95.00
Points to Ponder	11016	$ 29.95
Principles in Action	11019	$ 19.95
Success Factors in a Standards-Based Classroom	11017	$ 75.00
Teaching and Learning in the 21st Century: 2nd Grade Writer's Workshop	11053	$ 95.00
Teaching and Learning in the 21st Century: 3rd Grade Science	11047	$ 95.00
Teaching and Learning in the 21st Century: 4th/5th Grade Writer's Workshop	11048	$ 95.00

Other Products

Title	Order #	Price
Mentoring in the 21st Century® Resource Kit	11028	$ 985.00
New Teacher Professional Development Kit	11046	$ 795.00
Instruction for All Students PLC Pack	11051	$ 799.00
Meeting the Needs of Diverse Learners PLC Pack	11052	$ 799.00
Poster Pack	11006	$ 16.95
Visual Tools: The Complete Collection CD-ROM	11041	$ 375.00
Visual Tools: Meeting the Needs of Diverse Learners™ CD-ROM	11040	$ 100.00
Visual Tools: Instruction for All Students™ CD-ROM	11036	$ 100.00
Visual Tools: Leading the Learning® CD-ROM	11039	$ 100.00
Visual Tools: The 21st Century Mentor's Handbook™ CD-ROM	11038	$ 100.00
Visual Tools: Why Didn't I Learn This in College?® CD-ROM	11037	$ 100.00
What Do You Do When... Cards: Mentoring and Supervision Scenarios	11032	$ 49.95
What Do You Do When... Cards: New Teacher Challenges and Concerns	11050	$ 49.95
Scavenger Hunt Cards: *Instruction for All Students*™	11044	$ 10.00
Scavenger Hunt Cards: *Why Didn't I Learn This in College?*®	11045	$ 10.00

To Order

Call
800-940-5434

Online
www.justaskpublications.com

Prices subject to change without notice

Fax
703-535-8502

Mail
2214 King Street, Alexandria, VA 22301

Order Form

Just ASK Publications & Professional Development

Ship To

Name _____

Title _____

School/District _____

_____

Address _____

City_____ State_____ ZIP_____

Email _____

Telephone _____

Fax _____

Bill To (If different)

Name _____

Title _____

School/District _____

_____

Address _____

City_____ State_____ ZIP_____

Email _____

Telephone _____

Fax _____

Order #	Title	Quantity	Unit Price	Total Price

Please attach a sheet of paper for additional products ordered

Subtotal

Shipping and Handling
$6 S&H minimum per order
15% on orders under 10 units, 10% on orders 10 units or more
$49 S&H for each resource kit

TOTAL

**Contact us for quantity discounts and special offers
Call 800-940-5434**

Payment Method (Select One)

☐ Check (Please make checks or purchase orders payable to Just ASK Publications)

☐ Purchase Order   Purchase Order Number _____

☐ Credit Card   ☐ Visa   ☐ MasterCard   ☐ AMEX

Name as it appears on the card _____

Credit Card # _____

Expiration Date ☐☐ / ☐☐
Month   Year

☐ Check here to receive information about Just ASK workshops, institutes, and train-the-trainer opportunities.

**Mail or Fax to:
Just ASK Publications
2214 King Street
Alexandria, VA 22301
Fax: 703-535-8502**

Leading the Learning